CEO
POINT BLANK

Straight Talk for CEOs, Business Owners, and Entrepreneurs

ED JENKS

INDIE BOOKS
INTERNATIONAL

ISBN: 1941870015
ISBN 13: 9781941870013
Library of Congress Control Number: 2014952275

Designed by Joni McPherson, mcphersongraphics.com

INDIE BOOKS INTERNATIONAL, LLC
2424 VISTA WAY, SUITE 316
OCEANSIDE, CA 92054
www.indiebooksintl.com

TABLE OF CONTENTS

DEDICATION

Okay, so most folks who take the time to sit down and put some words on paper have a flowery dedication to their wife or mother like they wrote the next Moby Dick. I don't pretend that this is the next coming or anything and to be truthful, I don't think it's worthy of my wife. But my hypocrisy knows no bounds and so I will succumb to the norm and dedicate this whatever-it-is to my business partner, one of the world's premier behaviorists, and my best friend; all who happen to double as my wife Sharon. Here's why. Most people say their marital vows once and then like everything else, they forget about them and go about their lives. Sharon doesn't. We've been rich and we've been poor (the latter mostly always my doing), we've been better and we've been worse (the latter mostly always my fault), and not one time, not even one small time without exception, has she ever complained or blamed me even when it was clearly my doing. I've given her so many causes over the years to kick me to the curb and yet she continues to be my number one fan. That's not to say that she doesn't get on my case because she isn't afraid to do that for a second. But she's also not afraid to let me challenge myself, my beliefs, my values, or my behavior until I'm dangling off the cliff with the noose tightening. Then very calmly and without blame or ridicule, she pulls me back up, dusts me off, and sends me right back out into the fracas. The best friends you ever have will go with you into the dark, with no visible means of escape. She's my best friend and she's a one-of-a-kind which makes me, the luckiest guy on the planet.

PREFACE

I think it's important to the reader to clearly understand several things when you pick up a business book like this one so that you do not waste your time or have false expectations. First, unless you're just looking for airplane reading, you need to understand exactly who the author's target audience is so I'll clue you in straightaway.

My target audience is the young up-and-comers who have a vision of sitting in the chief executive officer chair one day. Those kids out there who think that they have what it takes to walk tall in the C-suite environment not simply for the money, but because they think they have what it takes to be there. To these folks, I say, go for it. No one is going to seek you out, you have to make it happen with a lot of confidence and as much experience as you can cram into your young life. Never be afraid and never think that age has anything to do with intelligence; just keep your chin up and go for it.

I also thought about young entrepreneurs and young family business owners who are consistently tasked with fast growth and legacy building, who understand that success has its own rewards as well as its own consequences. While you are not your father or your mother, you may well find that the ways of the past might not work for the future and thus change falls on you to manage. Your family name may take you to the top spot but it will not make you invincible or worthy to lead an organization. I remind you that wealth and leadership do not necessarily run in parallel with intelligence, and absent great leaders the masses will follow the poor example just as quickly.

I did not write these words for the Fortune 1000 CEOs who already have the impressive pedigrees and the multi-million dollar no-cut contracts. Instead I choose the other 97 percent of the nation's business leaders who are out there every day working their tails off to manage their enterprise both large and small, to some level of success, who lead without a safety net and are still not afraid to take the plunge.

Finally I would tell you that advice is good for the person offering it and that this book has a lot of advice, so make of it what you will.

CHAPTER 1

So You Want to be a CEO?

The 2000s, in my opinion, have been the most trying and difficult times C-suite executives have ever faced in American history. Yup, even tougher than the Great Depression. Not only do we have a tougher business climate, we are faced with bigger competitors—global competitors that do not operate under the same set of rules as we do in the United States. The idea that globally things are "fair and even" and "may the best managed company win" are concepts and beliefs shared by no one I know.

The global economy and unfair competitive practices aside, we continue to legislate and regulate ourselves internally to the point where we spend the majority of time wallowing around trying to create some kind of competitive advantage out of thin air. I spend a lot of time thinking about exactly what happened to us as a country post World War II when we were filled with hope and confidence that when all else failed we could outwork you. I see great companies struggle with trying to find production efficiencies while their foreign competitors are allowed to flow products into the American market unchecked and unregulated.

I must admit to being part of the problem. Here's why.

Post World War II, our economy was made up primarily of family businesses that covered the range of our needs from food to clothing, transportation, and manufacturing craftsmanship. Family businesses were passed down from generation to generation with the "secret sauce" that made the products or services unique to the region or geography they served. You knew where your food came from, where your clothes were made and you even knew the name of the family that made your car.

Our returning hero's average age was twenty-six and many were returning to the family business, or turning to trades they had learned while in the military. They were received into the workplace with open arms and the country was ready to step on the gas, fueling the largest generation of consumers the United States was ever to see.

The returning veterans were schooled in the family businesses and the discipline it took to operate them. They were charged with learning the tasks and craftsmanship of their trade because their mission was to protect the family homestead and their families relied on them. Those that had new talents put them to use still with the idea of making America stronger and their lives better.

The results speak for themselves. Some of the strongest financial years in America were from 1945 through 1965.

And then things got tweaked. Our foreign policy became unpopular. The average age of an infantryman in Vietnam was twenty-two. Our youth (I was one of them) rebelled against everything that even resembled someone telling us what to do.

Belonging to anything was frowned upon. I remember being at college one fall and seeing a group of guys spray painting a sign over a fraternity house door that said, "It's wrong to belong." We had begun to question everything, believe in nothing but freedom—whatever that was—and reject the foundational pillars that had given us the best economic conditions in the history of the world with the highest standard of living yet to be experienced.

It took a few years for the rebellious students of the 1960s and 1970s to get around to work, as most of us went to college, and many on the six year plan. As we began to assume positions of authority, we slowly began to bring our rebellious nature to the workplace. We threw out tradition. We didn't need to wear a stinking tie—we worked better in flip flops. We worked in cubicles because offices created "silos." I remember listening with rapt attention to one of the long-haired business gurus of the time with a prime time audience tell us to break down the silos, that big oil was making too much money, and the banks were ripping us off. He had all the answers. Get your people a meditation room—that's what attracts the real talent.

We all drank that Kool-Aid and we changed the face of American business just as we had changed the face of American culture fifteen years prior. The results speak for themselves.

Please understand that I am not accusing, because I was part of that movement and I was a leader at the C-suite level. As I look back at my career, I always felt like something was missing. No matter my success, I always felt a bit hollow. I think back on my college days and wonder why I didn't buck the trend and rush that fraternity.

We had all lost our business discipline. I could make money; that was the easy part. But I couldn't control my attitude and approach to anything that resembled authority and control, and believe me, I wasn't alone. Everyone was stupid, no one could keep up with me, and I wanted to run ahead of them and demand they keep up with me. Rules were for other people, not for me. I was so good at the money making part that most of the time, people would leave me alone because they knew inherently that they were better off for me running off like a mad man and putting money in their pockets.

So, here I am at sixty years old, having lived life well, still discovering and facing the truth about myself and looking to be better for it. I came to realize I have two goals yet to accomplish.

First, I want to be the person who finds a way to get through to other C-suite executives and prove to them that silos work, we can be competitive globally, it is okay to be a leader, and that the single greatest gift you can bring to an organization is discipline: order overlaid with a huge dose of forgiveness. If we are to bring our economy back to any level of dominance, we must be disciplined in our approach and willing to subjugate ourselves to our mission.

I have not been idle since my last engagement. In fact, I have done some of the best thinking of my life. When all is said and done, I have found six indelible qualities that we need to regain if we are to bring this economy back to any degree of ease.

I began to poke around a bit about credibility when I came across an article about a military special operations unit that had rescued two people that had been grabbed by some bad guys in Northern Africa. The story was an incredible tribute to a team of Americans who selflessly, and without any fanfare, put their lives at extreme risk by jumping out of an airplane at 15,000 feet, moving stealthily through a war zone undetected, finding the proverbial needle in a haystack, engaging the enemy at close quarters, protecting the hostages by laying on top of them throughout an extreme firefight, and extracting them from harm's way.

This one story was my answer. I had the material, but I needed a way of delivering the message that was credible and experiential enough to make a CEO listen. I found the Navy Special Warfare Unit, or as you know them, the Navy SEALs. Arguably the best trained task-to-mission instructors in the world, they exude confidence and credibility that can only be derived from experience gathered with personal discipline in an extreme team environment.

With their help, and a lot of luck, I created a program that brings into focus the need for discipline and order in American business. We do this in a rough-and-tumble environment where the lessons learned often come with a dose of reality that cannot be experienced in any other training venue. Spending a day in executive training with the SEALs is a day spent that will not soon be forgotten. (If you think your team is up for the challenge, you can find it on my website under S.O.S.T.) Hopefully my contribution to this effort will be worth the time.

My second goal: I want to be a CEO again. I want to sit in the driver's seat one more time before I hang up my briefcase, my United Airlines Red Carpet Club membership, and my three cell phones. I feel renewed, I feel like a better person, and for the first time in my life, I feel like all the holes are filled up. Gaining the benefit of discipline, both personally and professionally, at sixty years old is like getting another crack at winning the lotto. So if you have an underperforming portfolio company, or you're tired and want out, or you're just motivated enough to see how someone else might do it, give me a shout out. I'm an easy guy to find.

I took the liberty of changing names and in some cases timelines as it serves no purpose in content to expose folks I've worked with to my perception of reality. I have been fortunate to work with some incredible organizations and some incredible people. I do not for one second kid myself into believing that they were all excited to work for me or with me, but I selfishly hope they all learned something from the experience.

Being a chief executive is like no other life experience; it's a thrill no drug or activity can replace and you either love it or don't want anything to do with it. We are not mysterious creatures. Most of us have souls, and contrary to the general opinion of most people, the majority really do want the best for our organizations, the folks that work there, and the shareholders that believe in us. We have feelings beyond greed. Most of us are not overpaid for the responsibility we carry, and we do lose sleep over terminations and downsizing. There is not a day that goes by that I do not spend time re-thinking careers that have been lost over my decisions and the cost of decisions that I've made in terms of both human and financial capital.

This book is both case study and advisory and it is written for a specific community: those who envision themselves sitting in the top organizational chair. If you are tentative and unsure if the top is the right place for you, please understand that it is not my intention to scare you away, but rather to inform and advise you of some of the challenges you may encounter. Men and women who choose this career path are driven to it, and no matter what I write, they will believe they will be better than me, won't make the mistakes and most likely will read the book for entertainment, but not because they feel they need to. These folks are the "Type A", "High D" driven people who cannot be stopped by anything. They will make decisions quickly, recover if they make a mistake, and what they don't know they'll learn. They will outmuscle you if they are challenged. Most of these individuals have great oratory ability, are extremely quick on their feet, and most important, don't know how to be in a room without being the leader.

My journey has taught me many valuable lessons. For those of you who want an opinionated insider's survival secrets for being a successful CEO, read on. Let your journey begin here.

CHAPTER 2

You are Hired to be Fired

I've been fired a few times, as you can probably imagine. It's rarely fun and there is always some drama around the event. But rest assured, you do come out on the other side about 99 percent whole. My biggest issue with getting fired was actually not about the end, but the beginning: I was always hot to get going and since I loved challenges and turnarounds, I was so eager to get into the action that I was taken advantage of.

I'm not looking for any sympathy. It was always my own fault, and due to my own stupidity as it happened more than once. I would sign anything to get going and in many cases, boards do not have great counsel who really want to take the time to work through any issues you might have. They typically will delay an agreement or they wander around for a bit and then present you with the same agreement your predecessor signed, which may not necessarily suit your needs.

CEOs, like football coaches, don't retire. They always get fired. That may be an overstatement and I will get a bunch of hate mail from those characters that have been a CEO at the same place for a hundred years or something. So I will qualify it a bit. For those of us unafraid to lead change in aging institutions, who must grapple with people in key positions who have tenure all their own, and are willing to take on the challenge of financial deficits and uncooperative teams, know this: in the end, we go out as we came in. We get fired. Everyone loves us on the way in because we're going to fix things up and make their future more secure. But once you do that, and in the process begin to demand productivity and accountability, you're just a pain in the ass to people and they are not afraid to speak up about it.

First piece of advice. Wait. No matter how anxious you are to jump in and get started, wait until you're operating under a contract that protects your interests now and in the future. The first point you compromise on is the one they will nail you on every time. I've seen really senior guys get nailed on a simple expense account issue. Remember, Al Capone didn't get hit for the countless number of heinous crimes he committed; he got nailed for tax evasion.

So what do you look for? How do you know what you need? There are many things to consider and I strongly suggest you get yourself a great human resources attorney to help you. You want someone who works on the other side of the corporate line—the kind of attorney who, in other circumstances, might be asking you some tough questions. This doesn't have to cost you an arm and a leg if you're prepared when you walk into his or her office.

By the way, in these kinds of situations, I far prefer and recommend you hire an ass kicking female attorney as in almost all the human resources litigation fracas I've been in, opposing counsel invariably is female. They seem to talk the talk better and also, in the majority of cases, they are talking to corporate human resources which, in my experience, is predominately where you find female executives.

Being prepared for meetings with counsel means knowing what you'd like to have in your agreement that speaks to any concerns you might have. I encourage you to write it down and do not start creating the wheel when counsel hits the time clock to start. Attorneys are great listeners because when they are listening to you, they are making money, and attorneys always follow the money. They will let you talk all day if you want to as long as the meter's running. Make the ticking meter count and prepare yourself, including for the time it takes to communicate your desires. There is no story telling necessary to communicate facts. Also don't lose a major point here: Every CEO should have personal counsel that stays with you throughout your career. He or she should understand your motives, your idiosyncrasies, your style and should help you in crafting an employment agreement that works. Once you engage, your attorney should be kept up to date with any compensation and/or performance reviews (or the lack of same), and any other correspondence that you feel may at some point come back to harm or question you. When you get in a jam, and you will, you don't want to be playing dialing-for-help or worse, trying to convince a new attorney that you're a good guy or gal.

If you're going into a hostile environment, or if you're going into an environment hostilely, you want a contract that basically says, hey, we all understand this is already hostile so you can't come back later on and whack me when someone gets upset. There are always people in organizations who are upset about change. Where your predecessor might have let them slide a bit on meeting objectives, or let them take Friday afternoons off, you don't, and therefore you eventually will become a thorn in someone's side. This can come back on you later and you want to be protected against these kinds of issues or potential allegations that come with the territory. Your initial "friendlies" rarely last a month. Your help and decisiveness, that everyone loved the day you walked in, are often soon forgotten.

You also need to think carefully about a parachute of some kind that keeps you going if someone pulls the plug on you. Most contracts for the top executive will carry some sort of buyout clause. People get sick of you, the board gets sick of you, whatever, you need to establish how much cash you have to have in order to complete the timetable of transition. There are several tricks here. Most attorneys will want a two-step out; the first for "good reason" or "no cause," and the second "for cause." If you think you ever get a shot at the former, good luck and God bless you. Boards always want to terminate you "for cause" and if they can get something that sticks, you lose your ability to negotiate a safe exit and you'll wind up fighting them in court or in arbitration. Your contract should maintain the same financial deal whether you go happy or you go being dragged down the hall on your ass. Setting the stage up front while everyone is thrilled with your second coming is a heck of a lot easier than it is when the chips are down and you are, too. Remember, on the day they hired you they made the best decision of their lives, and that enthusiasm should work to get you the best deal for your exit on the day you start.

Inevitably, they also forget whose muscle and prowess created the changes that allowed them to grow their career, increase their revenue and make those bonus numbers look good. When you begin to turn up the heat on performance and quality of work with senior executives, you become persona non grata real fast. Get a contract and keep it contemporary to your needs, contemporary to the general business climate, and above all, contemporary to the current human resources legal indulgence, which is a constantly moving target.

Another key point is to establish a travel and expense policy that meets your needs. Write it, take it to the board, have them ratify it and publish it with human resources, the controller, your executive admin, and your audit team. When I say write it yourself, that's exactly what I mean—write it yourself. It doesn't have to be perfect, but if human resources touches it two things will happen: first, it will take months to get a simple policy written, and second, trust me, it will not be what you want.

Your company travel and expense policy needs to be written in accordance with your needs. No one in the organization understands what you do every day and also what you can't do in order to do your job. Waiting in line at the Department of Motor Vehicles is most likely not the greatest use of your time. (But sending your admin will come back to bite you later unless you have his duties spelled out in the policy.) Neither is sitting in the back of a small plane trying to find wi-fi and unable to open your laptop all the way because the guy in front of you put his seat back and is snoring happily away while you're trying to get down the terms of a deal you just agreed to. People don't get it. They don't get that you haven't seen your wife or family in three weeks because you've been in four countries on two continents. There is a reason why they created first-class seats and I always expected, both of myself and the executives who worked for me, to use flying time as work time. The challenge is most people don't understand what you do and most never will.

Make sure that the board expects the best from you and also for you. This means you don't always have to say who you had dinner with or who you met with in Los Angeles. There are so many examples of how this seemingly small issue can really hurt an organization that it's critical to your success, and the board needs to understand why.

I was really having some concerns over a CFO that I inherited with a turnaround assignment, and I was looking for a new one. In the course of searching, I had dinner with a recruiter that specialized in retained searches for CFO talent. I turned in my receipt for the dinner and my admin inadvertently put the name of the recruitment firm on the back of the physical receipt. It didn't take fifteen minutes after my admin turned in my monthly expense account with receipts attached that my CFO was in my face, shaking his fist and getting all kinds of shades of red. He of course knew the firm and surmised why I was meeting with them, and he was right. It was not a happy parting.

To really emphasize my advice, at one point I was actively interviewing candidates to replace two board members that had way outworn their contribution to the organization. I had polled my executive team to discern their thoughts and we were all in complete agreement. I set off on a journey to find suitable candidates. This required both travel and dinners, which at that level were not at McDonald's. Through some condition of fate, the board became aware of my actions and before I could act, they did. In my exit interview, one of their claims "for cause" was that I failed to accurately record who I met with and where I met them. In the interview, I refused to name the folks I talked to or where I was. They called this insubordination and added it to the list of "for cause termination."

Depending on the size of your organization, there also may be competitors that you meet or visit from time to time for a variety of reasons. I've always found it interesting that I can sit down with my competitor counterparts and have a great conversation without breaking one corporate secret or giving away any pricing or market share information. At the C-suite level, you can talk about industry challenges and laugh about common customers that attempt to play you off each other. It's always fun to meet someone who does exactly what you do at exactly the same time and with basically the same resources. My feeling has always been that you have to know your competitors at the highest levels and take the time to visit with them.

In one job I had, a commodity-driven product, where I went and who I met with had the potential to move the market, and not always in a positive way. Keeping my travel quiet and not always telling everyone where I was going was critical to my success, and in one instance, critical to the entire industry. I once bought my second largest competitor in a multi-million dollar transaction and we held that confidential until we closed the deal. If anyone in the industry had known what was going on, there surely would have been all kinds of challenges and issues raised which may have nixed the deal. You can have the control you need to keep a deal in play when you know which additional in-the-know staff to include in the deal, and when to do it. Whisper one thing to the wrong person and you can be standing before a Senate subcommittee explaining your intentions.

Be sure your travel and expense policy allows you to move with stealth, and act to your station which may mean expensive nights out with potential execs, or flying first-class with the folks you're making a deal with, or buying someone an expensive gift or a bottle of wine. In short, if your board trusts you, you need to spend what you need to spend to get the job done. Having such a policy in place helps the board remember the agreement when it comes time to part ways. But don't bet your life or career on it.

I was at the end of one of my contracts as a CEO and I was making a pile of money. I really didn't like the business much— short margins, fickle market, poor supply chain, you name it, this business had it. I'd done a good job getting things cleaned up from a governance perspective and I had spent a lot of time and energy building up some marketing steam. Early on in my tenure, the marketing team wanted to try some media promotions, but as usual, we didn't have the budget to shoot some video of our suppliers for their website and in-store promotions. I had a son studying at Loyola Marymount University in the communication arts program and he was struggling to make ends meet. I called him and told him my dilemma and as I expected, he quickly volunteered for the job. He and three of his cinema buddies rolled around the United States, sleeping in their cars, writing scripts on the road, dragging a van load of camera equipment through all kinds of weird places, and they shot tons of film. They were able to produce four one-minute commercials that were not only commercially acceptable, but speaking as a guy who's bought media his entire life, they were outrageously clean, funny, and marketable. They were so good that not only my company used them, but the entire industry used them. They did all of it for a few thousand dollars that didn't even cover their materials, only because their old man asked for help.

Four years later when I was negotiating my departure, the board in its infinite wisdom, wanted me to pay the fee back because their auditors couldn't find three competitive bids for the work, so they called it nepotism. Even when you help people, they forget.

There are times when you are forced to play the heavy and lead some very difficult terminations of some very senior talent. It is not fun and I don't think you ever get good at it. It is the one responsibility that cannot be entrusted to anyone else and it requires incredible fortitude and empathy. Firing someone in anger never works and typically causes consequences beyond the termination. Enlisting the assistance of human resources can be helpful in outlining the individual's options for COBRA and final payouts for earned vacation or paid time off. In many cases human resources can assist with employment agency referrals and in some situations can even provide letters of recommendation. That being said, in senior executive terminations, I would never allow human resources to act as the lead communicator. That's your job.

There are many ways to facilitate terminations and I have seen a lot of varying responses to the ultimate conversation. I can tell you that if a person is shocked by the final conversation, you haven't done your job properly. I do not believe that the termination of any individual under my leadership came as a surprise, as this would have been the culmination of many conversations in which I would have expressed my level of dissatisfaction with the job performance, the attitude, or the skill set. I'm not saying I am or was a perfect leader, nor am I always saying I was right in the decision to terminate an employee. I am saying that it was my responsibility to facilitate the termination based on my interpretation of the current conditions or of the individual's performance. Right or wrong, it was my job to directly communicate that information to the individual.

For senior executives that had tenure, right or wrong, I always tried to give them a lot of notice. In many cases this meant giving them several weeks or a month on the payroll during which time they were free to pursue interviews, speak with potential employers, or engage with recruiters. This allowed them to tell their families and create their own chatter about their circumstance. I have received a lot of criticism for this approach but thus far it has never backfired on me while allowing those individuals the dignity of walking out the door. No matter the circumstance, it is and has always been my policy to give everyone the dignity of walking out the door with their head up, to allow people at that level to say their goodbyes without some security guard or several office workers packing up their stuff and walking them to the door. If you have done your job properly, they already know their credit cards have been shut off and their computer access changed before the conversation so a more public flogging is not allowed in my wheelhouse.

I'm quite sure human resources would disagree with most of these recommendations and I'm sure the counsel for human resources would strongly disagree, but there are times when doing what's right is more important than doing what may not be perfectly to the letter of the law. As CEOs we sometimes walk a very fine line when it comes to human resources issues and some of the most critical decisions we make are around employment issues. My advice is to follow your conscience and try not to hurt anyone more than the termination itself will. Adding insult to injury serves no purpose, no matter how poor the performance or circumstance.

Once I had a very experienced consulting CEO tell me that he tried facilitating turnarounds but that he got no pleasure out of being a "hatchet man." Although I have gone into many organizations that needed aggressive leadership to dig them out, I have never acted like a hatchet man and never have I felt the need to throw all the executives out on their asses. The majority of senior executives, even in situations where the company is not doing well, are not poor performers. My experience has shown me that people can step up and do great things if they have skilled, educated, and experienced leadership that helps them focus their energy on the right things. I have also, in my years, solidified a pillar belief that some people have a "size niche" that works for them and many have a difficult time transitioning beyond that size. Here is just one example of many that I have experienced.

At one point in my career I was asked to help with a medical device company that was growing in spite of itself. It had a great concept of the razor-razorblade model and also was providing a very contemporary solution to a large issue which meant its consumption community was "ginormous." The challenge this company was experiencing was that the engineering group who had been so successful at developing this product mechanically was having an extremely difficult time building throughput into the manufacturing process.

The company had invested millions of dollars into a new production line with one-off custom made equipment that should have easily been able to handle production. The problem was, it didn't work and seriously, the room was dark except for one engineer that reluctantly tinkered away at it. Production continued on two old and outdated manufacturing lines where all the engineering talent was focused on trying to keep the old equipment up and operating. When I asked the director of engineering why he wasn't focused on making the new line work, he shrugged me off saying that it was best to keep things going on this line where his engineers knew what they were doing.

This is what I call the size dilemma. The engineers, and specifically the director of engineering, didn't particularly care if the company grew as long as they were comfortable with what they knew and produced a quality outcome. They were always excited about developing new uses for their product and prided themselves on supporting incoming concepts and ideas from sales. Their research and development team was overflowing with ideas and projects. The problem was they were disappointing customers who couldn't get delivery of their razorblades.

The director of engineering was very comfortable in a fast paced research and development environment and really enjoyed interacting with his engineers to keep equipment he originated and designed going. He would take hours explaining one small piece of assembly to his team and did so with great pride. He didn't want this old equipment to go away and was quite content with knowing every screw and pneumatic in the system. There was not a chance in the world that he would work to get the new line going and that is exactly what I told his CEO.

Once given the task, and to make a very long story short, within thirty days I had the new line up and operative, delivering four times the throughput of the old lines combined. In two more months we had engineers trained, standard operating procedures in place, throughput was crazy hot, and people were jazzed about production. While the director of engineering initially got excited with the production, it wasn't long before he opted out and went to work for a start-up company that was asking him to build some custom equipment.

The moral of this story is that some people are comfortable with a small family-owned enterprise while others want to work for Google. Some folks are comfortable in organizations with a hundred employees so that they know everyone, while some people like to get lost in the masses. As a CEO, I often had to terminate employees who, by no fault of their own, had been left in the dust by an organization that had simply outgrown their comfort zone. Conversely, I have also hired people that I thought would work out who had experience with larger organizations only to find that without the support of a super structure, they couldn't function in a smaller entity. I often wished I could have that conversation with folks and have them agree and understand why they had to go. Unfortunately I have not found many people who could accept that line of reasoning.

In any event, when the end is there, and there is always an end, try not to wallow around too much in it and never allow the mud to stick to your feet.

CHAPTER 3

The Making of a CEO

Before I tell you how to get where you want to go as a leader, let me share where I came from. I was born in a small, rural community in southwestern New Hampshire in the early 1950s. The son of a devout Catholic girl from New Jersey, and an atheist style New England hard case. My mom was raised in New Jersey with a big band of brothers and sisters and a considerably extended family. They worked hard, studied their faith even more and trusted the lord for forgiveness. My dad was from a broken home, had distance between all family members and enlisted in the Navy just as World War II broke out. From that point forward, he was never the same.

My dad came back from World War II, married, and took his new bride to New Hampshire, where he would build our family home, and he went to work as a draftsman. He was undiagnosed for more than forty years with post-traumatic stress disorder and was an alcoholic from the day he returned home from the war in 1945 until the day he died at seventy-seven. He had one nervous breakdown, and a number of alcohol related illnesses including a heart attack at sixty-two. My dad had few if any friends and I can never remember my mom and dad ever going out together. They didn't go to parties, they didn't have friends together, and our family vacations were always spent with relatives in New Jersey.

My first exposure to business was through my dad's slurred speech every evening denouncing his company (where he worked for thirty-five years), his bosses, the owners, and his work associates. He was unappreciated, they all cheated to get ahead, and when they did get ahead they turned right around and screwed him. No one was trustworthy, no one worked as hard as he did, and no one realized how good he was. He held a very loud and direct conversation with himself every night recounting the number of times people had treated him poorly today. There was little good in his world, and he hated the business of business.

I had three older sisters who were close in age and they still live happily in the hills of New Hampshire. They are successful in their own right, school teacher, international commodity buyer, and sales rep. All pretty normal and still collective as a family, while my mom, the consummate matriarch (now ninety-three), lives with my youngest sister, still goes to church every Sunday, drives a new car I bought her last year, and contributes to chores around the house.

Every single night from as early as I can remember, my dad came home and drank himself to the ground. On countless nights I dragged him to bed until I got old enough to pick him up and carry him. In my entire life I never had one meaningful conversation with my dad. We never shared any intimate moments, he missed both my high school and college graduation, most sports games I played in, and my wedding. The alcohol was just too meaningful to him and as I grow older I've come to understand this illness and even with awareness it is difficult to forgive. His advice to me was never go to college but join the military and go to Vietnam, be a man. When I went off to California in 1974 to get married he told me not to do anything illegal, gave me twenty-five bucks, and walked away bottle in hand.

He and my mom had little substance to their relationship and with her deeply devout religious beliefs, my mom would never consider leaving my dad, yet at the same time never would force him to receive the help he so desperately needed. I can remember her crying many nights after I put my dad to bed and encouraging her to pack our things and leave. She just couldn't allow herself to be more concerned with her own well-being than she was about her marriage and it was her belief that she should support her husband no matter what. Even at that age, I knew my mom gave her life away. More important, I knew I would never give mine to anyone.

My solace was working, for no money of course, on a family farm in town. This was the kind of New England farm with the big red barn and silo, horses, cows, chickens and everything you would expect to find in a rural farm community. The family who owned the farm took me in, as they did almost anything that strayed down the dirt road. They fed me well, included me in their lives as easily as if I was a feather blowing in the door. That was to be my safe haven and sanctuary for almost eight years and I was as common to their table as anyone else in their family. It was a place where I would learn the art of deal making and the value of negotiation.

For eight years I watched the haranguing of old New England farmers as they swapped, traded and negotiated their way through fancy chickens, horses, cows, produce, the odd sheep or goat that passed through, and even an occasional ruckus over a car or truck someone wanted to swap. It was not uncommon to see the price negotiation on a prize rooster continue well into the night, punctuated by homemade libations, until two old guys would settle for a quarter. It was a place where I would see the same people negotiate a similar transaction hundreds of times and no matter the previous outcome, always come back to the table anew and ripe for the next trade. It was a place where laughter and practical joking came easily, no one asked a lot of questions about my dad, or why I would be waiting on the steps when they came out to milk cows at five o'clock in the morning. They just accepted it. That of course and the fact that I worked like a demon for free didn't hurt. In my entire life on the farm, I was paid $100. But the value in saving me and teaching me how to live life is, as they say, priceless. That farm is the only thing I miss about New Hampshire, though I went back once and no one recognized me. But that's another story.

I graduated from Keene State College in 1975 with a science degree in education. I don't know how I graduated as I was a horrible student who rarely cracked a book and tested poorly. It was the tail end of the love generation and I probably got a lot of "gifts" from professors who were having their own private revolution against the establishment. I recall one professor who handed out As to anyone who only came to his first and last lecture. He got fired eventually but not before I took every class he taught. I would come around later in life to be an attentive student and a great believer in lifelong learning, but in 1975 I was a college graduate with not one hope of getting a job as an educator. I had a new wife from California, and when the bell sounded on graduation day in May of 1975, I walked to my Ford Pinto, got behind the wheel and never looked back.

California was a real education for a kid that had never been out of New England. My wife was born and raised in northern California, the daughter of an extremely wealthy immigrant family who owned a bank and a number of other holdings. They were world travelers and there were many nights when I attended dinner parties with astronauts, politicians and well-recognized world figures. I listened to what they talked about, how they carried themselves, the stories they told and the expectation of wealth that is a common thread among that privileged class. I was a pauper with a poor education, and could not add one thing of interest to a conversation. I could not have found Greece on a map for a million bucks and these people knew the adjoining islands and the people who owned them. I wanted that life and I wanted to become involved in the conversation. I wanted to participate in life rather than react to what happens next; I wanted a plan to get there.

Over the course of my twenty-four year marriage, I would see multi-million dollar deals get made, I would see how strong ethnic ties are more powerful than education, skill, and experience combined in having the opportunity for wealth and leadership. A whispered word here or there and the son or daughter of a friend would get a job, have an opportunity, be included in a deal or in many other ways be rewarded for being in the right family. In strong ethnic families, I learned that family, blood family, would always be excused their shortcomings and supported no matter the digression.

My wife was an illustrator, an artist, and a really good one. If you have ever perused a book rack in any store in America, you have seen her work. While this is a tough and challenging career where only the best survive and few get there, the money is hardly sustainable. It took years and years of school and tutoring for her to reach the pinnacle, and all the while someone had to pay the bills. That was me.

My first job in California was working for a moving company. I was moving seven individual social security offices from around the states into one building in California in a massive consolidation project. My job was to push a fully loaded filing cabinet on rollers from point A to point B. The next man was to load the roller from Point B into an elevator where it would find its space in a long line of others just like it on the next floor up. I was working as a scab for a highly unionized moving firm and I learned a lot about how unions work. Most of the time when I pushed my cabinet to its destination at Point B, the next man ignored me. If I left the roller there and went back to get another one, the union supervisor would yell at me for creating a back-up. So, my only solution was to push the roller all the way into the elevator and run back as fast as I could to get another. This doubled my work and forced me to ignore the union worker who was happy to watch my antics and collect his pay voucher. But I never got yelled at again and I was one of the few scabs that made it through the entire move and was asked to stay on full time and join the union. I didn't.

This experience crystallized my first foundational belief, because heck, when I thought about it, I had been doing something my whole life that always worked for me. I worked really hard. I got up early, I worked like a dog at every job I ever had, and I never could get enough hours. So my first self-described life lesson was simple: outwork everyone.

So I'm twenty-one and married, I'm living in my in-laws house, I am not of the same culture so I do not speak their house language, and they have two daughters and two sons. Translation: I am the odd man out and if you have ever been in a situation where everyone speaks their native language when you come around, you got to know something's up. Further translation: They hated me. I spoke funny New England English, had long hair, no money and no career. In the summer of 1975 I applied for more than a hundred jobs and didn't get one call back. I once went to San Jose for an interview at the city recreation center only to find out it was a civil service test in an auditorium with 500 other people applying for one job. That's what a college degree bought you in 1975.

I finally worked up the courage to ask my father-in-law for a job. Something temporary of course, until a teaching job opened up. Now my father-in-law couldn't just give something to anyone. It had to be accompanied with a lecture and conditions. Sometimes the lecture would have relevance about his higher level of consciousness, or the importance of loyalty (to him), or sometimes I just couldn't understand his point at all. But through it all, the one thing I realized was that as he saw it, the world revolved around him because he was at the top of the food chain and he wanted you to know it. So he gave me a job repossessing cars for a lease company he owned.

As it turned out, 1975 was a good year for repossessing cars. The economy sucked, banks had overindulged, and leasing cars and equipment was the new way to live the dream. No money down, loose credit terms, car dealers writing the contracts and it didn't take long before the deal imploded. Repossessing cars can be fun and very challenging, especially when the car you're trying to grab is locked in a garage or the person knows you're coming to get it. In one day in Los Angeles, I grabbed four Jaguars from a gated commercial parking garage from the same dentist. I excelled at repossessing cars. I would go anywhere with no more than a license plate number and come home with a Cadillac Coupe. I was in California, living the dream. I moved out of my in-laws' place and into a little bungalow in Piedmont, had a few pennies in my pocket, and always an expensive car out front. I was living large.

The point of outworking everyone is pretty basic but where this first life lesson manifested itself for me would only come into my vision later in life. Early on I created a habit of going to bed early and getting up early to get to work. This allowed me to roam my work space without restriction, study equipment up close, stand on the line where manufacturing took place or go to the board room and practice my presentation. I could actually read the mission statement on the wall, I could read all the notices on the employee bulletin board and I could look at the charts for sales without interruption. I would get there earlier, stay later, volunteer for every project, get on a plane, a bus, or drive anywhere I was asked to at any time. I would attend any seminar I was sent to and sit in the front row and I always asked the most questions. I would find the guy or gal who had the longest history with the company and sit with them for hours while they told their stories. If I didn't know as much as you did the day I walked through the door, within weeks I would know more.

I have maintained that principle throughout my career and to this day it is still contemporary to me in both concept and outcome. While words and notions of balance, life synergy, work life presence, etc., sound good in theory; it doesn't work if you want to sit in the driver's seat. As a CEO, you don't get down time, you don't get privacy, you don't get to get lost for a week, and you are never forgiven your sins, and we all have them.

THE IMPORTANCE OF CRITICAL THINKING

I spent the first fifty years of my life thinking that I had not learned a thing from my dad. In fact I spent more time wishing he had been someone else and what I had missed out on than taking some time to try and understand the man. My dad was a semi-functional alcoholic from as early as I can remember until the day he died and as I said earlier, we never had even one meaningful conversation that would help a young man gain perspective on a future.

My dad hated the people he worked with including the building, the owners, the equipment, his projects, his boss, his co-workers and overtime. They were mean, they had everything while he had nothing, the sales people were all crooks and liars, his boss was stupid and got promoted for all the wrong reasons, and the owners were wheeling money out the back door in the middle of the night and by God if only they let him run things he wouldn't be the way he was.

Once when I was being interviewed for a talk show and the woman interviewing me asked me why I saw things differently than other executives; what caused my career to take me to the C-suite and ultimately to the chief executive seat when other better educated or more experienced people were available? At that moment, in that flash of a second, with that one question from a host whose name I can't even remember, I saw what my dad had given me. He had given me the gift of critical thinking.

My dad questioned everything, deeply, and he believed nothing. With that as my constant example, without one word ever being spoken about it, he had given me something that people spend thousands of dollars trying to get (and rarely do) and years of study trying to figure out: the innate ability to see even the best situation critically. That was my "Aha!" moment. The real trick, however, was to not be critical of the situation, the people, the organization, or even the outcomes of all or any of those actions; that was something I had to learn to do myself.

I relived that moment not long ago when my wife and I were having dinner with a prominent financial guru and having just facilitated a stressful yet successful organizational turn, he asked me the same question, "Why are you able to do what you do?"

My wife, knowing this is a question that absolutely embarrasses me like no other, answered for me. She said, "Ed just sees things differently." She said it so matter-of-factly that it plausibly answered the question. I spent the rest of the evening running that through my head and trying to come to grips with it.

Allow me to explain how I see things differently.

Let's say we go to the county fair. There is music, there is excitement, there are rides, food, animals, shows and exhibitions. There is a lot of unusual noise and movement, some anxiety, perhaps, over the scary rides. You are overwhelmed by the senses of sight, smell, taste, hearing and touch. Everyone is focused on the in-the-moment experience—the fun, the bright colors, the laughter and the camaraderie. Everyone that is, except me.

On the way in I noticed that there was no premier parking. There was space but it was a service not available. It would have been worth double the normal parking rate. Tickets were not sold online, thereby creating a relatively long ticket line. The owners tried to mitigate wait complaints by having a colorful band playing upbeat carnival style music at the entrance. Nice, but paying one more ticket attendant and getting people into the fair to spend money was far more valuable than paying a bunch of musicians whose music still did not solve the lengthy wait to enter. (Mental note to see if the COO of the operation was competent.) It was a hot day and once inside the gates, you had to walk all the way through the mid-way to find bottled water. (Mental note to have water vendor near front gates.)

I could go on and on like this all day long without the need or desire for any kind of mental break or the need to carry a notepad. I can be a grandfather, help my grandkids walk around the fair, go on rides, have lunch, enjoy the shows, almost everything that everyone else does. The difference is the recording device in my head never shuts off and the internal commentary just keeps going on and on and on. By the time I was there an hour, I could see tens of thousands of dollars of lost revenue, underutilized staff, wasted space and opportunity upon opportunity for improvement—all without being negative for one second.

My wife will tell you that she has to repeat everything twice; that I am often detached from the experience at hand, and that I overanalyze everything. She will tell you that I can easily miss the emotion of the moment, and that I am incredibly hard of hearing, and always preoccupied with my own thoughts. She will also tell you that I can fix things faster than anyone she's ever met, that I can figure out just about everything, and that she's never met anyone that other people can rely on more for positive outcomes.

I was recently asked for some help by a very young entrepreneur who had found some growth money in the form of venture capital from several medium sized venture capital firms. He was having trouble with his board and the communication was not going well for him. The board agreed to speak privately with me to see if we couldn't work out some issues. They were gracious in terms of complimenting him for his technological skills but not quite so complimentary on his communication ability. They wanted to replace him. I agreed to attend a board meeting to see how things shaped up. In the first board meeting I realized that although the resumes for these new directors were strong enough to field a reunion at Harvard, when you dug in a bit, there was no real operating experience. In today's environment, it is not uncommon to have an entire brigade of financially centric directors and a token executive with operations experience making up the dynamics of many corporate boards. All the financial participants naturally want a seat to protect their interests, which doesn't leave a lot of room for operators.

The challenge of the board was that the young entrepreneur founder was a brilliant technologist, but like many of his contemporaries, he had never actually operated a business. In this company, without experience managing the sales channel, things often got away from him. In this case, that meant that he lacked the focus of defining a target consumption community and sticking with it. The result was constantly overpromising and under-delivering on the gross revenue side because the CEO kept moving the target from minnows, to sharks, to whales, and never actually brought any into the boat.

The board's reaction was that they loved the idea that the fledgling was attracting the interest of the whales and they encouraged the bravado and expense of going after them. This lasted two more board meetings until a private investor meeting was held and a discussion of the credibility of the young entrepreneur was called into question. This was not a question of credibility. This was simply a question of helping the company identify their optimal consumption community and then having the sales team focus on landing those target clients rather than changing the target in hopes of making up revenue lost. Some quick advice and sound pipeline tracking processes quickly put the entire team back on track. The board went from wanting to replace the CEO to getting excited about working on pipeline analysis. The ability to be critical without being negative offers CEOs incredible leadership advantage and this skill always translates to successful outcomes.

Seeing things differently has offered me a completely new perspective on my dad. In recently trying to put his career together, I am getting to know him better and trying to understand the complications that made his life what it was. Clearly PTSD played a major role in his outcomes and outlook and while it traumatized his life, it has helped mine. Maybe that is the most unselfish gift a father can leave his son.

CHAPTER 4

Early Lessons: The Formative Years

I did wind up leaving my bank repossessing job after working my way up the chain to collector, customer service rep, and finally credit officer. Banks are interesting places to work; they are regulated to death by the government and yet they still get confused. This is not difficult to figure out as the customer care is performed by low level talent while most institutional banks are so top heavy with overpaid talent that it takes a room full of them to make even minor lending decisions. There always seems to be a lot of drama in banking and if I learned anything in my banking tenure, it's that you really work hard to find the folks who don't need the money and then you press them hard to take it.

That being said, there is no better place for young people to grow careers than banking. In addition to learning about finance, credit, and collecting money, there is an incredible benefit in that you see such a variety of business, jobs, and people. Everything about banks is about making money. They do this through simple fees that when applied to the masses offer huge returns to the shareholders. After two years in that bank reading personal credit applications and a wide variety of profit and loss statements from various companies trying to borrow money, I had a front row seat in the University of Bank, and I was a good student.

I had made a list of who made the most money (attorneys, hands down), what companies had for assets, who kept a lot of money in the bank, and what companies struggled every day to make payroll. This made a significant impression on me as a young man because I had no intention of taking off on a journey to a place where I would have to struggle along with a struggling company. While I was not strong enough to always heed my own advice, I have been careful not to hang around with companies that are cash strapped. When I see an aged culture that is founded on loyalty that means "please hold your paycheck till Monday," I'm gone in a second. It's unhealthy for everyone and that kind of cultural loyalty is a fleeting compromise to your long-term mental health and certainly to your financial health.

Later on in my consulting years, I would ask my audience or training class to raise their hands if, in their careers, their employer had bounced a payroll check to them. To this day I am still amazed at the number of hands that go up, and I can tell you it is far more than 50 percent.

In 1979 I realized banking was probably not my thing and I began looking for other opportunities. I had grown my understanding of finance and credit exponentially and for the first time in my life felt like I had a skill to parlay on the street. I tried a small business (retail sporting goods-every young man's dream), and barely escaped with my ass after losing money for three straight years. While it wasn't much money now, it was my entire savings in 1979. At that same time we hit the worst recession in almost forty years, fueled by an oil crisis that had us backed up around the block to fill our gas tanks. At one point I was paying 19.5 percent on my revolving line of credit and the rest is history. I sold the company in 1981 for pennies on the dollar and barely got out of there without filing bankruptcy. From that experience I learned that capitalization is everything and without capital, real money to spend, there is little if any chance for success. This would prove to be true over and over again throughout my career. Large or small, aged or start-up, you have to have your hands on a lot of cash.

The biggest danger in throwing in as a key executive with a cash-strapped company is that there is nothing—and I mean nothing—that takes top talent off their game more than money troubles. It stalls creativity and forces you to live in every aspect of the organization, compromising for even the most simple of needs. You will put up with poor performers because strong performers don't need the hassle of worrying about their payroll check. You will compromise your supply chain because you will deal with second tier suppliers who charge more but give you longer terms or second tier products to work with. And one thing banks really know how to do is sock it to you the second you lose any status in your finance vehicles.

If you find yourself owning a business like this, you really need to take a hard look in the mirror and figure out how, and if, you can turn this thing around. And if you can't, you really should move earlier rather than later. It's a hard lesson to learn, especially when you have poured the family savings into your idea or you've invented a product or service and you just can't make it run fast enough.

I was working in a company once and I had a friend who I would sit on the back porch and drink beer with on weekends and shoot the breeze. He was a really smart guy and he worked for a big shipping line and he was enormously successful. I loved talking with this guy because he thought of things I never even dreamed of. After a few weeks of hanging out he stopped coming by. I saw him at the store one day about halfway through the summer and asked him where he had disappeared to. He asked me what I was doing and of course, I launched into my latest dissertation about what a difficult time I was having getting this team to work together. He finally put his hand up and smiled and said, "You know something? Sometimes you get on a team and no matter how hard you work or how hard you play, they just can't do it. Move along and learn, or make yourself crazy. Or continue to make me crazy listening to you which isn't going to happen." He turned around and walked away and for the first time in my life, I did too. Hanging out with teams or businesses that can't or won't perform isn't good for you or them and you can't associate walking away with defeat. It is what it is.

In 1981, I took a job that would put food on the table, allow me to have a lot of fun, and take the summer off. I went to work in the ski industry (every young man's second dream). I worked for a large foreign manufacturer who had purchased a successful American-based ski and ski boot company and was looking to expand their US market share. I skied more than eighty days in the winter of 1981 all over the country and at the very best resorts you can imagine. I was learning to be a road warrior, and learning how to sell; both life lessons that stay with me to this very day. To sit at the top, you have to be willing to travel hard and still get your business done quickly and efficiently. If you're the kind of person who needs to sleep in your own bed every night in order to function adequately, you're not going to sit in the top seat long.

In my opinion, sales should be a prerequisite for all CEOs. I'm not saying that every CEO has to be Zig Ziglar or Tony Robbins; you can hire people to do that. But you do have to be comfortable with people and comfortable relating to people on the assembly line, in the executive suite, and everywhere in between. You need to be the first one to offer a greeting, you need to remember people's names and you need to be able to memorize the details of other people's lives. You need to be able to relate to the ten-dollar-an-hour single mom who's busting her chops every day so she can go home and raise her kids to be decent people. You need to understand how brand new employees feel when they don't even know where the washroom is, and you need to be sensitive when someone is having a difficult time. And you need to be able to make this look easy.

BACK TO THE LIFELINE

They spared no expense in setting up this company and were relatively hands off once they selected the new CEO and president. The new president, our fearless leader, moved west from New England and had that preppy, school boy kind of look and the attitude to go with it. Horn-rimmed glasses, full head of wavy hair, dressed in topsiders and khakis with his Lacoste shirts and a sweater casually thrown over his shoulder even on the hottest of Los Angeles days. The interview process was fun, as disjointed as he was, and probably today would be totally illegal, but interesting for me. I was accepted for the job, a regional salesman in California, Nevada and Arizona. In our very first meeting in Los Angeles in 1981, he pulled me aside and said that I had to trim my mustache because you couldn't trust people with facial hair. Feeling like a jerk, I went to my room and cut it down to acceptable size.

My mustache has been my trademark brand for forty years; it's big, it's fat, it sometimes changes colors, and it fits me and my personality. I've only shaved it twice since I was sixteen years old and regretted it both times. But the lesson here is that when an employer does something to people that makes them feel bad about themselves, it's probably the wrong place to work. In one of my gigs as a CEO, there was a large number of kids coming into the workforce with tattoos covering their arms, necks, etc. While I'm not a tattoo guy myself, I always cared more about the job you did between eight and five. Rather than change the policy and leave a significant number of qualified kids unemployed, I asked my team to accept this as an age wave thing. When I went out and spoke to that department one day, I complimented one of the girls on her ink. It wasn't my thing but she and her boyfriend loved this way of expressing themselves. I can tell you for a fact that after that one talk, they worked like crazy people in that department. They never turned down a challenge, they supported change and they walked the talk. Learning to accept idiosyncrasies has always worked well for me and in this case, accepting a little ink got my customer service team on target and on time.

Most leaders will take passive employee performance as status quo rather than push for breakthrough thinking and aggressive, questioning talent. We don't like the guy or girl who calls us out on our strategy or our focus because they challenge our stability. As a CEO I loved them like my own kids; their brashness and courage would always take you to places you would not have been able to reach and I didn't give a crap for a tattoo if the guy or gal wearing it was a star. I have the capacity to overlook a lot of shortcomings or alien differences to my own point of view if you are really good at what you do. Valuing human capital is becoming a lost art among leaders in the United States, and you could argue that it was legalized to the point of extinction with the human resources legalese that overpowered American business in the late 1990s. Sexual harassment, hostile work environment, employee grievances over lack of perceived equality; those issues neutered leaders in such a way that it has become impossible to enjoy the spontaneous nature of celebration or reward relationships that benefit enterprise.

When more than 70 percent of Americans date in the workplace and 50 percent meet their marital partner at work, how in hell do you police that activity? I've found that if you put someone in a place where they can be honest without recourse, they will be honest. Conversely, if you make things fear-driven, where they will receive the worst consequences if they are honest, people will lie. I know because I did, right along with the rest of the 70 percent. When you're just starting a new job, you always find those (or they find you) who have the dirt on everyone from the cleaning crew to the executive suite. They always find a way to get you alone no matter how hard you try to avoid them. These people are masters at working at any level and still being alone with you in the elevator, or finding you at the bus stop in the rain, or standing next to you at the urinal. They initiate conversation to get your attention and then they find a way to lay a bomb on you; something that makes you think you knew something only to have this person tell you otherwise. This water cooler kind of culture can permeate an organization to the point where it becomes a dysfunctional and unpleasant place to work. One of my first tasks in any organization was to create a zero tolerance policy for this horrible behavior and the first time it happens, one termination usually lets everyone know you're serious. A good friend of mine who is also an experienced turnaround leader summed it up quite succinctly once for me. He said every time he picked up his keyboard, all the little cockroaches would come wiggling out and he eventually would have to whack a few to let the rest of them know he meant business.

Pete comes to mind when I think about an absolute master at being a cockroach. Pete was thirty-five and well known as the company gossip. He was gay but not yet out of the closet and he had a wife that he hid behind most of the time. It was one of those unwritten rules that no one talked about but everyone knew. As a result of his personal inability to lay out who he was and live his life happy, Pete was always trying to deflect potential criticism by openly laying everyone else's laundry out on the table. Pete made it his business to know yours and at just the most inopportune moment, he would slide you easily in front of the train. In the time that I spent on that engagement he was a complete nightmare and he was still there when I left. Like the proverbial cockroach, he had a way of surviving through all the turmoil and somehow coming out ahead, always at someone else's expense. No matter how much I encouraged Pete to live his life true to who he was, he just couldn't do it. By being a victim himself, he upset the entire office and constantly contaminated everyone around him and thus controlled the show.

So the topic, and the job, becomes about dealing with difficult people. Why are some leaders more successful at this than others? Why do some organizations seem to be above any personal trauma and exude a culture of confidence and purpose? The successful CEO never lets the craziest person in the room dictate the day.

HERE IS MY EXAMPLE

You and a group of friends are spending the day in the city enjoying the sights, doing a little shopping and taking in the culture. As you're walking down the street your group notices that there is a person ahead yelling and screaming and threatening everyone who walks by. What do you do? You quickly move to the other side of the street to avoid any unnecessary confrontation. The lesson here is that the craziest person in the room typically controls the day. As a CEO, weeding through those folks is your job and making sure they don't control your business is job one.

THE ANXIETY EPIDEMIC

Early on in my career, I suffered horribly from anxiety. It was completely debilitating, worsened by the fact that I remained undiagnosed for years and was left to my own methods for dealing with this terrible and intrusive disease. That's the down side; ultimately, it has become my strongest asset.

In 1973 I was working forty hours a week running a county program for the recreation department while also attending college full time. The work load was crazy and I had little time to myself. I was stressed over making ends meet and trying to keep my grades at a place where the dean would stop sending me nasty letters. My job was to supervise athletic programs for the handicapped youth in the area which primarily meant those ambulatory but not mentally functional folks. I coached basketball and bowling programs, participated in training for Special Olympics and ran the general day-to-day coordination of transportation to and from events and programs.

This was a high-stress job in terms of attention to the detail of each and every participant, ensuring that they were safe and not going to hurt themselves or someone else, as well as making sure that they remembered to go to the bathroom and maintain good sanitary health. In this position, it was never as simple as hopping in the van to go somewhere; there was a whole list of things you had to do before that was even a possibility. While I enjoyed this work as one of the most rewarding contributions to others I ever have experienced, it was still extremely stressful.

I was really excited one weekend to actually have from Friday night to Monday morning completely free of any responsibilities, either for the job or for school. I had been interested in this really pretty girl who lived and went to school in Boston and so on Friday afternoon, I hopped a bus to Boston to spend what I thought would be a great weekend with her. I was probably there for an hour when I got hit with my first official anxiety attack: couldn't breathe, fuzzy vision, uncontrollable shaking, etc. My friend took me to the local emergency room where I waited in a complete panic state for several hours until finally the doctor came in. The doctor took one look at me and asked what drugs were in my system. I told him I did not take drugs and never had, which caused him to shake his head and tell me to come back in the morning once I was "straight." For the record, I did not then, nor have I ever taken drugs of any kind.

After I started to breathe again, I was still left completely debilitated by my condition. Riding the bus back to New Hampshire on Sunday, I was a wreck and thought I was losing my mind. Once home, like everything else I have ever done, I began to study my symptoms and I devoured every book, white paper and textbook I could find that talked about my symptoms. In the fall of 1973, I diagnosed myself as having chronic anxiety disorder induced by sleep deprivation, over-work and stress. Thus began my journey to recovery.

Anxiety is a strange companion; I found controlling the physical manifestations of the affliction to be manageable; controlling the internal mental state derived from the disease was the most challenging. In talking to a number of physicians from various disciplines over the course of my life, no matter how much study one put in on the subject, I could tell in a second the ones who also had the personal experience of anxiety. Those were the professionals who helped me the most because they really understood the feeling of the disease.

At first, I practiced control of the shaking, profuse perspiration, and breathing by taking control of small bits of time. I would say to myself, don't forget to breathe and hold your hands still for ten seconds. I would remind myself that I was in an air conditioned room so there was no need to sweat. Gradually, a few seconds at a time, I could gain control of myself until over the course of a year, I was completely free of any physical symptoms. But my battle was less than half over.

The mental crisis that accompanies an anxiety attack is scary because it does feel like you are losing your mind. You float and race through every negative thought you can imagine and most importantly, you stop trusting your ability to be happy and engaged with what's going on around you. Your instinct is to get out of the situation any way you can.

After my continued self-education on the disorder, I began to confront my symptoms with a best case/worst case scenario. I would walk myself through each negative thought and allow it to run its course which was always a world ending catastrophe. Then I would re-run the same thought, but condition myself to a different outcome that was both positive and rewarding. Rather than run from myself or my negativity, I allowed that experience to happen and then changed it to be the way I really wanted things to be. Since this exercise was all run in my head, I could practice this control anywhere and at any time I chose. Thus it all became about control and more specifically, self-control over my state of mind.

Over the next decade, I became mentally and emotionally strong beyond what I was born with, all due to having gone through one incredibly dark and potentially debilitating disorder. This mental strength, born from dealing with anxiety disorder, is one of the greatest assets I possess as a business leader. In situations that might cause others to lose their confidence in direction or decision, or perhaps even to question their own ability to persevere under stressful situations or extreme duress, I never lose a beat and I never fail to engage.

Having confidence in your own ability, even when everyone around you is in a panic, or in strong discord over your stated direction, action, or belief, remains the single greatest asset a chief executive brings to the team. Where you get that strength and confidence is based on your skill, education, and business experience as well as the full set of life experiences you have had, including some that might be derived from dark places.

CHAPTER 5

It's All About the People

Here is a riddle.

Picture a conference room with a meeting underway. There are twelve chairs around the table and eleven people in the room, leaving one empty chair. With this information, how do you tell who the CEO is?

If you answered the person sitting next to the empty chair, you solved the riddle. It always fascinated me that people naturally do not want to sit next to the boss. Occasionally you'll get a brave soul, but it will only last until another player gives him or her some crap about kissing up to the boss. It moves equally to an extreme when you attend a dinner with your team. This happens for a lot of reasons. Some don't want you to notice that they consume large amounts of alcohol, or that they are texting their girlfriend all night, or even that they might not enjoy your company. What a novel concept. Many times I wanted to shout, "I don't like you either and I'd really like to be home with my wife rather than out with you assholes!"

I've also run into my share of those who walk the road less traveled. I was facilitating a high-level strategy session in the southern region of the country with a high-end technology company. This was a well-run, second generation, cutting-edge kind of organization that could advance concepts quickly and had a great platform for adding services. In my pre-session discovery, I kept getting strange vibes from the executive team members. They were all young, boyish looking kids, including the CEO, who had recently purchased the business from his father and was an extremely capable engineer.

I went into the strategy session, an off-site meeting some distance from the company's headquarters, with sixteen key executives and director level personnel. This was to be a two-and-a-half day strategic planning session and this was something that came so naturally to me that it never felt like work. That said, I was not feeling like I had the entire story here.

The first day went off without a hitch. There was good discovery, common information, and a good historical look at themselves. While they had an incredible platform, a great technological leader who had its engineering practice down cold, their sales were just not getting any traction and they were not able to leverage their platform. In fact, a competitor with more money but less intelligence was gaining some ground on them and creating a large threat. I planned to dig deep into the sales program on day two and I was already forming some ideas about how to help them.

That evening, they invited my colleague Sharon and me out to dinner with the team. Sharon, a behaviorist, and one of the best in the country, usually worked with me on these sessions taking teams through experiential exercises she used to break up my business modules. Besides giving them and me a break from my rather direct and pounding style, she had them teaming up and working together to solve some really interesting mind benders that help me better understand how the team thinks collectively.

I usually have a strict rule that we do not engage in any outside evening plans with our clients and we rarely have dinner with them. Instead we retreat and let them blow off some steam without having the resident consultants hovering about. But something was bugging me after that first day, and I wanted to watch these guys in a lighter setting to see if I could figure it out.

It was one of those hot muggy southern nights and my clothes had been stuck to my body since early morning. I was sweaty and my voice was raw from talking all day. The only thing I could think of was an ice cold beer and Sharon was right there with me. We were late arriving at the barbeque joint and the team was already there, laughing and joking. Sharon and I slid into a booth and when the waitress came up to the table to take our order I said, "Two of the coldest beers you can find, I'm parched."

In an instant something changed. All conversation ceased, even the waitress stopped dead in her tracks and simply stared at us as though she was seeing a ghost. In several moments of extremely awkward silence, Sharon and I locked eyes and it was like a mutual, did you do something? Did I do something? Is my zipper down? I did remember to put pants on, right?

Eventually conversation started back up, our beer came, and we placed our dinner orders. Shortly thereafter, the vice president of sales slid over into our booth and said very quietly, "Now you know what I'm up against." As we were to discover over the course of the evening, and well into several years of good consulting work, the owner and the overwhelming majority of employees were strict religious folks who did not drink, dance, play cards, smoke, or in any way engage in activities that they did not consider to be in line with their beliefs. Admirable qualities for sure, and since the team all carried the same beliefs and values structure, it worked well for them.

That being said, one of their biggest challenges was that their competition was known as the party kings and queens of the industry and would drop anything to take you out for a weekend in Las Vegas, or on an exotic vacation, if you were in their fold of customers.

What did we learn from this adventure? Well, the fact is if you want to sell into mainstream America, you've got to either play the game or be happy with less than. We eventually encouraged this company to hire a vice president of sales that had an expense account where he was permitted to entertain clients in a more mainstream manner. They wound up leasing an office for him in California and rarely invited him back to the corporate office. Business picked up, and today they enjoy a majority of their industry market. I don't credit their success with wining and dining clients; I credit their success with removing roadblocks that allow them to achieve their goals without directly sacrificing their culture.

The big lesson here, however, is much broader: it's always about the people. There are some very basic rules that a CEO must follow in order to fully understand the organization and although they are simple, failing to execute on any one of them will ultimately spell disaster. The building of relationships and the process of building relationships within the culture is the most important job a CEO faces. I recommend five simple steps in building effective relationships with your team. They are:

1. **Contact:** You have to get out and meet them individually and it has to be in their arena, not sitting across from you in your office which can be the most intimidating seat in the house. Walk into their workspace. Give them the opportunity to show you their space and their support staff. You make no progress sitting in your office all day waiting for them to come to you.

2. **Commonality:** This should be baked into the system, but the fact is you are first together to do great work and this should make finding things in common relatively easy. The trick here is that it's up to you to relate to them, not the other way around. Finding something in common with others, even if it's only work related, is paramount to successful relationships that are enduring.

3. **Credibility:** In training sessions with young executives, I always use the same lesson. I put my hands in front of my face and moving them from one side to the other, I advise that every time you see a person, they are judging you as credible or not credible according to their own sense of value. It's a bit of a dumb lesson mostly because there have been those moments where I have not had any credibility whatsoever. That aside, you have to be able to do whatever it is you say you can do in order to have credible relationships. We do know however that one case of "not

credible" for a CEO can spell disaster. Being credible over and over again is what supports enduring relationships.

4. Confidence: This is pretty simple. Kind of. If you are offered enough opportunities to be credible to your team, eventually they will begin to follow you even if they are scared, intimidated, or unsure. Initially they will follow you because you're the boss and they have a greater fear of being fired than following you, but as the relationship grows in credibility they will follow you because they believe in you.

5. Trust: Remember in the previous point when I said they would follow you? When the relationship begins to be even more credible with time, you are not afraid to let them lead the way and they are not afraid to step out and become leaders themselves. That's the ultimate success level for an executive team. As a CEO, you will be lucky to have that experience even one time in your career, but you should never stop looking for it.

THE "GAME CHANGERS"

I recently wrote a new program for the consulting side of our business called Strategic Operations Skills Training. The premise for the program is that there are six what I refer to as indelible skills you need to have down cold if you are going to thrive in the C-suite. In order to deliver these disciplines with intense credibility, I needed some credible instructors. To make a very long story short, I exclusively use United States Special Warfare personnel to facilitate this program. (Those are Navy SEALs for those of you that are new to the jargon.)

There are many reasons why using Navy SEALs works really well in this program. As I conducted the program over and over again, there was one thing (among many) that jolted me out of my normal daydreaming self. It was a realization of something that I had always tried to define for the purpose of finding the kind of talent that they brought to the equation. Hanging out with these guys day after day made me realize that one thing. Big or small, loud or quiet, style aside, every one of these SEALs is a game changer. Not one of them can walk into a room without making an immediate threat assessment and creating an immediate action plan in their heads. As a result of the incredible training and discipline they inherently bring to any situation, they have a confidence that is unmatched by any other group of humans I have ever hung out with. They are not afraid of anything or any situation due to the commitment to the mission, the constant training, an inherent interest in successful outcomes, all coupled with a mental and physical toughness that is extraordinary.

When I think about it, the folks I have worked with that I always gravitated to and proactively wanted to support and help, fit the same style of character. They were all game changers. These are the folks that can't wait to get into the office to see what the day will bring and what they can make of it. They are actively engaged, always interested in another point of view, and see opportunities in every situation they are in. They are also scarce; perhaps even ready for the endangered species list.

While this is a takeoff on the theory of hiring the best talent you can find and surrounding yourself with people smarter than you, it's hard for many CEOs to be comfortable walking this talk.

After my experience working with the SEALs where the example is just so visible and real, I have changed my entire approach to interviewing talent. I now look at a potential candidate first to see if they have the skill, education and experience to do the job and once that is vetted, I move the interview forward to discussions on confidence, the ability to dream with purpose, and the integration of skills with organizational strategy. I not only look to see if the person sitting in front of me is an organizational game changer; I want to know if they have the ability to change their industry.

Think about this when you look at your executive team or your department employees and ask yourself if there are any game changers on the payroll. The biggest trick here is to ask yourself with complete honesty, Am I a game changer?

CHAPTER 6

Finance

I don't know how many times I meet executives who are on a career path they hope will take them to the CEO chair that, in early coaching sessions, will confide to me that they don't really understand finance. In further discussions, I find that many of them do not understand an income statement and fail miserably when talking about balance sheet performance.

If you don't understand these basic tools of business management, you will definitely not fare well in understanding the complexities of the various number of financial vehicles used to fuel growth that are readily available to CEOs today. The best advice I can offer is to get your tail back in school and work to gain not only an understanding of this most important function of your job, but a mastery of it. I am not talking about becoming a tax or audit expert; I'm not talking about committing a lifetime to becoming a CPA. (That's what your chief financial officer does for a living.) I'm talking about a mastery of managing growth, combined with managing expense, understanding how the business functions financially, and how the key operating indicators are influenced by associated financial levers. You need to understand when things are out of whack and what needs to be done to get them back on track.

A great CEO understands how to protect assets, how to use debt, how to leverage existing infrastructure to gain economies of scale, and when the balancing act of having enough working capital to be opportunistic while not constricting short term debt availability is swinging away from reason. It's important to protect current assets and it's important to understand return on invested capital so that you can see well in advance when you're going to need new equipment and facilities.

Managing your CFO is, I imagine, something akin to trying to manage the Pope, because as good as you think you are, the CFO is typically looked at as the most honest, if not the smartest person, in the room. To a certain extent, that's the way it should be as long as you don't abdicate your responsibility for fully understanding finance, speaking directly with your audit firm partners, or intelligently engaging with your bankers. I always made a point of meeting with all outside financial support operations without my CFO from time to time. This let them know that I knew what I was doing as well as offering me a direct pipeline to the decision makers if the shit hit the fan and vice versa. As a CEO, you never want to totally delegate outside relationships to anyone; these can be shared but never 100 percent delegated.

Sometimes it's hard for the CFO to remember that you're the boss, as they tend to believe all decisions are and should be financially centric and everything else should come second. If that were the case, I never would have been successful, as many of the decisions I made were not managed well on paper but I knew I could manage the investment or opportunity and therefore was comfortable with the risk. For the most part, I always had good relationships with my respective CFOs and most of them would listen to my idea or concept and work to vet it rather than destroy it. That's not always the case, and if you have challenges with your CFO, you need to think hard about how to resolve the issues or move them on as there is no room for conflict between the CEO and the CFO.

I counted once and I think I have worked with nineteen different Chief Financial Officers in my career so far. They were as different as any nineteen people could be and I always found this particular position and the men and women in it extremely interesting. In many cases they were fascinating people. In contrast I think they all pretty much saw me the same way; loud, tough, demanding, unrelenting to prove my position and most likely, a general jerk. I was okay with that because it meant that they would work really hard to prove me wrong. If they could prove me wrong, I typically would listen and with new information, I would change my mind. This infuriated most of them, but satisfied me immensely and served the companies I worked with quite well. It was an internal check and control that I feel naturally goes with the two positions.

To me, the CFO was, quite simply, the Keeper of the Truth. This was the one position that most closely resembled corporate conscience and would keep things in governance perspective no matter what anyone else said or did, and that's exactly the way it should be. When you think about it, there are many times when a CEO has to be the cheerleader; that's when things aren't going so well. There are times when you might not be able to tell the whole truth and there are times when you have to play bigger and look stronger than you might feel or be at the moment. That's your job. The CFO always has to play the straight man to the CEO and good ones know when to shut up and when to exercise what I call the walk around the parking lot.

There are few people in the world that an aggressive CEO will take criticism from, and the CFO should be one of those people. I was fortunate in my early years to have one of the best CFOs and mentors anyone could ever have. When I came into the organization, he had already announced his retirement so I wasn't going to spend the rest of my career with him but I still got him to hang around for a couple of my formative years. Glen was a cranky old fart but he had paid his dues in a big way and was hands down the best CFO I have ever witnessed in all my thirty years in business. In his youth, Glen had been with a Big Eight accounting firm. He was a seasoned CPA, was an undergrad from Brigham Young University, had great audit experience, and knew the business of business cold.

My turning point was when I was in the annual audit meeting with our CPA firm and Glen, going through our year-end audit page by page. The room was really hot and stuffy and this meeting was b-o-r-i-n-g to a fault; I was close to nodding off when Glen abruptly called a recess. Walking down the hall to the men's room I felt that big hand of his close around my collar. He was not even close to nice when he asked me if I had the slightest idea of what that meeting was all about, and if I knew anything about what he was going through. I admitted, most likely flippantly, that I did not and we went back in and finished the meeting with him glaring at me and emphasizing his points loudly as if he had to work to keep me awake.

The next day, I had a voicemail on my office line from the admissions clerk for the Executive Immersion Program at Stanford University, inquiring as to what session on finance I wished to attend. Glen had an interesting way of not taking no for an answer and the night before, had called in a marker and enrolled me in the finance program. This was his not-so-subtle way of walking me around the parking lot and getting me straightened out about what was important. In our history together, we had three such walks and they were all humbling and extremely educational.

From that moment on, my life changed as a CEO. I began to not only understand finance, but I became an advocate for everyone on my staff getting deeply into the numbers and not just understanding the financial statements, but learning how to make them dance. After so many years of looking at the numbers, I must admit that I don't make a move without understanding everything I can and then asking as many questions as I need to in order to get the entire financial picture.

All that said, I was still not the Voice of the Keeper of the Truth; that always resided with the CFO. I have learned a few things along the way that may help you out in understanding the numbers as well as how to effectively manage the CFO and the finance team.

1.   **Get the most knowledgeable, experienced, and**

skilled CFO you can find. Pay them the money they want because they are worth it, and they will save your ass a hundred times if they believe in you.

2. Get to know your CFO. This is the one C-suite executive that it pays to have a good personal as well as business relationship with. This isn't always easy because they are, in many cases, quite different than you. Where you are spontaneous and opportunistic, they are often patterned, deliberate thinkers who want to take the time to see every i dotted and t crossed, vetted by hard numbers and numerous models before they are ready to play. Give your CFO an opportunity to do that; it will help both of you. You may sometimes feel this person is slowing you down—deal with it.

3. Get financials done early. Financial statements should be out and ready for distribution within seven working days of the prior month's close of business. Faster is better, but in my experience, any faster than that and the mistakes magnify by a significant amount.

4. Keep close to the CFO. Encourage (read demand) that the various business unit executives stay in close touch with the CFO, keeping her posted on any anomalies they are encountering before they hit the financial statements. CEOs and CFOs do not like financial surprises and they want to be in the know in real time all the time.

5. Vigilantly monitor expenses and revenues. Encourage (read demand) a 3 percent + or – performance-to-plan in all expense and revenue categories. One mark of a great CFO is to predict both near term and long range financial performance of your organization. The larger you get, the more your bankers and board want to see predictive indicators, and they want these numbers to be accurate in order that they can offer solid advice on the deployment of capital.

6. A CFO should love to model the financial future and should love taking your ideas and creative thinking and turning them into predictive outcomes. If you add new geography, new products or services, reduce cost, increase revenue, make an acquisition, sell an unproductive division, etc., a great CFO will listen, ask questions and without a lot of fanfare, come back to you with a bunch of "what if" models for you to chew on.

7. Have a plan B. Have a solid back-up plan for financial management and always have your CFO mentoring someone who shadows the position and has at least rudimentary knowledge of how your CFO operates. Continuity in financial reporting and management is critical to the internal operations of the business, but as important, constantly assures the bankers, auditors and market in general that things are okay.

Last, I am always surprised that the majority of CEOs and CFOs do not follow any particular economist with any regularity. I have always made it part and parcel to my job, to watch general economic indicators and the economists who predict them. Like anything, there are some out there who are not very good but they are very loud, there are many who are cautious about everything and really don't have an opinion on anything, and then there are some terrific economists who actually put their track record right out there for you to see and are exceptional at communicating their message.

I like the Beaulieu Brothers (Alan and Brian) from New Hampshire. They are straightforward and have a pretty good handle on things. Following their indicators, I am usually able to understand what's coming at me which allows me to align my strategy to address potential challenges.

I am often asked for references for professional services and I am fortunate to have direct working relationships with a number of banks, bankers, VC, IB and PE groups as well as attorneys, CPAs and consultants. As different situations require different talent, if you drop me an e-mail, I will do my best to hook you up with the right talent. I have a pretty good handle on strengths and weaknesses of professional talent as well as a general idea of fee structures.

CHAPTER 7

Human Resources and Corporate Development

In great organizations one of the biggest differentials is the gain you get from a terrific human resources department and its relative leadership. This is also one reason why there are not a lot of great organizations.

Human resources departments are rarely a great resource. I don't say that because I don't like the department or the function; I say that instead because HR is typically so caught up in the minutia that they just don't get an opportunity to actually be a proactive resource to anyone. My experience is that they are typically so focused on finding the lost paycheck, mediating differences between employees, straightening out a benefits snafu or caught up in the latest nuisance lawsuit to be proactive at any level. I have been fortunate to work with a couple of bright human resources stars, though there have been a lot of mediocre to poor ones. The challenge with human resources is that until the late 1990s, almost every human resources "professional" was the former secretary to the boss and inherently picked up all the human resources tasks as the company was moving from start-up to growth and beyond. The majority of these folks were not educated to their task and if they were, it was almost always on the job training. I call this group of human resources professionals the pretenders. They really don't have the skill, education or experience to help you get where you want to go and my advice is to avoid them at all costs.

Many certification groups did a reasonable job of helping these folks learn the basic concepts of human resources management and would offer short chapter studies on topics such as labor law, basic compensation, payroll, and benefits administration. While this education and the related certifications were certainly helpful, they were not designed to transition a secretarial pool clerk to the status of a C-suite human resources professional. In my years of consulting, I was always amazed at the lack of professionalism, knowledge, and leadership that was tolerated in this vital and important department. I was often left shaking my head at how otherwise bright, intelligent chief executives would tolerate mediocrity in the handling of employee matters and how they would ignore the potential fiduciary exposure and liability created by their human resources staff. This would never have been tolerated at the CFO position, for example.

In the early 2000s we began to see a new breed of human resources professional emerge from our universities and colleges that were well educated, contemporary, strategic, and good at what they do. These folks have changed the face of the profession and added vitality and long term vision to their organizations. They are participants in C-suite strategic decisions, can read and understand the P&L and balance sheet, and most have a solid understanding of labor law. These are the ones to look for. They are not cheap, they demand access to the executive team, participation in the vision and goals, and they demand access to the top. My advice: give them the time and include them unconditionally in your strategic vision and let them help you pave the road.

In the early 2000s I was working with a high-tech medical device manufacturer on the edge of Silicon Valley in California. The company was owned at the time by some investment bankers and the idea was to build the organization and sell it to a pre-determined target mother company in the same industry. Employees of course don't know these plans and rarely are they included in this kind of process with these kinds of financial owners. So, absent any concern for organizational culture, the owners were deftly tuned in to the operating matrix attempting to make the company as close to a mirror image of their target take-out partner as they could. A sound strategy in anyone's world.

I had been hired by the CEO to help facilitate some order to the inter-departmental meetings between production, sales, research and development, and regulatory affairs. Seems they were all very talented both individually and collectively but couldn't get along with the inside of a bucket. As I considered my approach, I wandered by the human resources office to see what insight I might gain before I walked into a meeting with a whole lot of people that I didn't know and that didn't know me. I wound up spending the rest of the day there.

Sally was an extremely bright woman and had been hired as

a contract human resources professional. Her credentials were impeccable. She had a solid ten year history of successful human resources consulting and when I met her that day she was ready to walk. Sally clearly understood the long term investment banker's goal of build and sell. But she didn't understand why they spent so much time and put so much pressure on operations and no time on cultural development. She knew employees were frustrated, and she knew there was significant discord between departments that was disrupting the ability to get products to market. She was also frustrated because the CEO wouldn't give her the time of day. Did I mention that Sally was paid over $150K a year?

So, let me get this straight. You buy yourself a really terrific gem of a human resources professional and you don't want to give her the time of day? I went back to the CEO's office with a very different agenda.

I'm not one to pull punches and I certainly didn't in this case. Cliff was one of those tall, tanned guys you'd expect to see at the gentlemen's club, an attorney by education. Self-absorbed, quiet, and extremely cerebral in behavior, he was the kind of guy who could spend all day by himself and be quite content. I admittedly opened up on him a bit and was straightforwardly critical as to the information he provided me in my preparation for organizational entry. He clearly was confused by my aggressive nature and I could see him spinning my words around in his head. He waited a few minutes and then very softly said that he paid the top wages in the industry, he hired only people from the most prestigious educational institutions, and he hired only the very best of the best talent available. His question to me was naive. Why should he have to manage relationships? He actually expected these folks to lead themselves, overcome conflict, make collective decisions and work out all their differences internally. It wasn't his people that needed help, it was Cliff.

Over the course of the next several months, we began to have meetings where we talked about how to make decisions and team leadership. We covered each other's goals and agendas and we had people actually talking to each other. Sally introduced a brown bag lunch program where teams could make short presentations to keep others up to speed on their projects. And slowly, the organization began to get some traction. Sally expanded her programs of inclusion and discussion. She started everything from health and wellness programs to a lunch time volleyball league. Given the support, Sally paved the way. In 2003, the company was acquired according to the investment banker's strategy and the first thing the new owners wanted to learn was how they had created such an open environment and such a solid culture. Sally was a gem.

They are not all Sallys. I was working one particular stint as the CEO and president of a rather stagnant and aged institutional company in the early 2000s. I had entered the business with the idea of helping them develop their organizational strategy. One thing led to another and I wound up in the top spot. From the start it was a disaster. The governance was so screwed up that of the five corporations the company owned, the majority of directors were either dead or not to be found. There was employee discord, there was shareholder discord, and there was always some kind of nuisance legal suit happening. The board consisted of some inside and outside directors who kind of played the game but were not terrifically productive or even involved. This made for interesting board meetings as the former CEO, who was still chairman, would not provide any information at all, the CFO would complicate matters by producing financial statements mixed in with operational statistics, and the meeting would consist of storytelling by the chairman, a huge catered lunch, and everyone would go home. They accomplished nothing and they divulged nothing.

The vice president of human resources had the additional title of "Corporate Development," an interesting twist but not uncommon to find the human resources position looking for additional stature. This was one of those human resources folks that I talked about in the beginning of the chapter: grew up in the company in general admin positions and was appointed up to the position. No formal education at all and no mentor in the organization to learn from so on the job training was also a bit of a stretch. At forty years old he had been with the company close to twenty years. Almost every issue the company faced could be laid right back on his doorstep. He was a nice person, but lacked the skill, education, and experience to fill his roll. It once took him more than eighteen months and tens of thousands of dollars in consulting just to publish an employee handbook.

Cory could spend hours each day either on the cellphone with his wife and kids or sifting through mountains of information on mundane and insignificant issues. He was challenged in a number of different ways but the most dramatic was his ability to lose track of priorities. As in all executive functions, the ability to set and meet organizational challenges in a timely and efficient manner is of paramount importance. Cory just couldn't do it, and it crippled the organization. His lack of knowledge in accounting, manufacturing, recruiting and training was clearly evident, which led him to become an expert in one thing: terminations.

While the overall company turnover was just about zero due to a high percentage of hourly labor, the rest of the company suffered painfully. In one year alone the company systematically hired, trained, and fired fourteen out of eighteen new sales hires, and Cory didn't ask one question as to what we were doing wrong. In addition, as icing on the cake, Cory loved gossip and he liked to talk to his pals about what went on in the C-suite. It got to be a joke with me that I would tell him a story in his office and by the time I walked back to mine, the information was already back to me. So you're naturally thinking, why did I keep him? And I get that question, believe me. In truth, it was because I had bigger fish to fry, as he wasn't the only one on that team with challenges.

So, storytelling aside, how do you find good human resources executives? The answer is simple: network. You spend time understanding not simply the functionality of human resources but what you really expect in the way of support for either cultural sustainability or cultural change. You boil those concepts down to meaningful goals that can be assigned, measured and managed. A great place to network is at a meeting of the Society for Human Resource Management (SHRM), a nationwide group that hosts or sponsors meetings and various themed get-togethers. It really helps to go hang out with these folks once in a while and ask some questions and meet some potential players from the human resources community. You will also be amazed at how your human resources executive reacts when you show up to one of these functions unannounced.

To illustrate an example of human resources engagement, let's see if I can be a bit more definitive. If your culture hangs its hat on a decentralized customer service program, and it was designed to put decision makers closer to the customer, that's culture. However, once you look at the financial statements and the cost of this customer service delivery, you might determine, "Hey. It's not working the way everyone thinks it is." Now you have a challenge in changing the cultural attitude to match good economics. Human resources should lead this charge by replacing one set of cultural beliefs with a new set of core values that employees can understand and agree with. I've seen many companies do things like this and yet only one or two were able to facilitate it correctly.

A great human resources leader would understand the need to change, find solid reasoning that would actually add credibility to the change story, develop a time-stamped delivery program for change management, and then train/reward, train/reward, train/reward. Sometimes teaching people new things sounds like training your dog with lots of repetition and reward and you know what? That's exactly how it works. People will respond positively to training and change as long as they feel like they have an honest chance at being successful. That means letting them know what's in it for them and then rewarding them for their efforts.

In this example, the outcome of the human resource contribution can clearly be measured in economic terms and accordingly rewarded. The cultural position can be proven to be less costly if customer care were consolidated, perhaps greater organizational continuity in handling similar customer issues, or the speed of response by the customer care team might increase, and the complaint log could diminish. All of these examples can easily be measured as financial outcomes.

Here is a checklist I've found helpful when assessing my current human resources executive and it also can be helpful in quickly evaluating a potential new hire.

✓ Do I have a professional or a pretender?

✓ Where has his career taken him? Benefits administration, compensation/payroll, HR generalist, HR executive, personnel manager, HR legal, what is his hands-on experience?

✓ Is she passionate about her career? How does she demonstrate that?

✓ Does this person understand and communicate in financial, goal-oriented terms? Can he or she read the P&L?

✓ Is this person proactive in introducing new concepts in HR or is he a protectionist?

✓ Does this person understand employee development? Can she give you an example of how she accomplishes employee development?

✓ What kind of culture is this employee most comfortable working in?

THE POSITION DESCRIPTION

Do not underestimate the need for role clarity and role definition, even for key executives that are paid hundreds of thousands of dollars. The position description should hold as much definition as possible of the actual activities the executive is expected to lead and participate in. This is where you can let detail run rampant.

You will find outlined below, a copy of three documents by which I assign, assess and evaluate in-place C-Suite executive duties. The example offered is for a CFO, but you will see that the outline would play the same for any of the roles. If you want further examples for other positons, give me a shout out via e-mail and I'm happy to share additional position outlines. I hope they will help you and keep you from having to reinvent the wheel.

THE TASK OF MANAGEMENT

The task of management is one of the most useful tools I have ever developed in helping to manage executives at all levels. In fact, I could go so far as to say that if I had been more diligent in the use of my own tool box, I might actually have been fired less frequently. Then again, I would not have had as much fun or as much opportunity had I not been. The task of management allows the CEO an opportunity to express how he or she sees the job as it relates to behavior, participation, and contribution to the organization as a whole. It allows the executive the opportunity to ask questions specific to the position, gain clarity on what the boss sees as essential duties and responsibilities of the job and together you can add to or subtract from the list as you develop your relationship, your skills, and your leadership place on the executive team.

STRATEGIC INITIATIVES

Strategic initiatives are both short- and long-term supporting actions necessary to achieve organizational goals. An example would be a goal of achieving overall gross revenue of $50 million in three years. A strategic initiative to support this goal might be to hire, train and deploy five new sales professionals to unproductive territories. The plan might call for a gain of two this year, two the next and one after that, making this a short-, mid- and long-term strategic initiative. There is reward potential in meeting these initiatives this year, next year and the year after and progressing to the goal. These initiatives should be under the control of the executive and everyone should understand what overarching goal it attends to, what success is, and what the reward is for its achievement.

These documents should be developed at the start of each year, reviewed on a quarterly basis, rewarded as often as necessary (and/or disciplined), and most importantly should always remain contemporary to the organization and to the economic conditions that are applicable.

Mr. E.S. Jenks, President/CEO
Newco Corp
1234 Main Street
Anytown, California 99999
Re: MBOs 2019

I have read and understand the attached Objectives of Management 2019, (MBOs), which represent the achievement necessary for me to receive my "at-risk" compensation.

Date: _____

_____

Mr. Joe Smith, Chief Financial Officer
Newco Corp

January 2, 2019

Mr. Joe Smith, Chief Financial Officer
Newco Corp
1234 Main Street
Anytown, California 99999
Re: MBOs 2019

Dear Joe,

The attached document represents the MBOs that I feel will best offer the company the opportunity to support a payout of your "at-risk" compensation. I have put a lot of thought and consideration into this document and in that light, you will see that I have leaned toward the continued development of both your career and the reformation of our financial reporting metrics as the primary focus for you in 2019.

While we are off to a rocky start in 2019, we cannot always look outside at the economy as the reason we are not successful, if we are not first being the best we can be internally. As you know, I feel very strongly that we have a long way to go in financial reporting to be considered a Level Five organization. The clarity in reporting we need to offer those that are responsible for sales and production must be constantly reviewed for use value. We cannot lose sight of the end goal which is enabling our teams to proactively control our financial well-being rather than report on it or react to it in history.

We do not lack for reports in quantity, yet our reports have not allowed us to enjoy consistency in market predictability. In the last few years we have enjoyed growth EBITDA but it has not been predicted in the categories for which we planned. Great care must be taken when this occurs as luck does not always win the day. The board is concerned that reacting to the market is necessary; however, predicting the market is even better, and relying on windfalls can be a real problem.

This year will require your focus on the detail of these reporting changes. This does not mean your sole focus, but includes the focus of your support staff to the detail in their projects, plans, and reporting strategy. Your major task is to ensure that the detail is communicated to your direct reports and peers so that they might support you in this effort. Taking the time to explain things is one of your greatest skills as a leader; taking the time to regularly do this will be of paramount importance. I strongly encourage you to call time when it is your meeting and the discussion centers around what you need to say and explain to executives, direct reports, and line staff.

In your desire to move forward with your career, I am making a part of your 2019 MBOs the completion of an emersion course. It has been budgeted and now we need to move forward with this. I believe the benefits will be significant to both you personally as well as the company. I encourage you to take this very seriously and work as hard at that course as you do internally for us.

I assure you that I do not take MBOs lightly and I can assure you that the achievement of these MBOs will not be subject to argument or discussion come November of 2019. I will not pester, pressure, or remind you of the timing of the delivery of my requests; off timeline and they simply will not be accepted. Offering me last minute arguments or after-the-fact explanations will not affect the payout of this "at-risk" compensation. Thus, as it should be, you will know every minute of 2019 whether or not you are "in-the-money" and you control your own outcome or income as it may be.

As we progress in our relationship, I continue to be impressed with your skill and knowledge about the business in general and Newco specifically. Your sense of dedication to its success is admirable, commendable and more than that, appreciated by everyone. After spending these last several years working with you every day, I am of the belief that you can achieve or exceed every MBO and TOM that I have put in front of you this year. I firmly believe that with your leadership and direction, we can move quickly through the majority of your MBOs and implement these important changes.

We have a lot of work to do, and we need to get to it together and without delay.

Cheers,
E.S. Jenks, President/CEO
Newco Corp

Joe Smith, Chief Financial Officer

Newco Corp

Objectives of Management Year 2019 (MBOs)

At-Risk Compensation Plan

The Task of Management: Finance and General Management

The MBOs for CFO Smith are found on the following pages. In addition to the 2019 MBOs there are expectations of general performance that require continuous and diligent attention. I define these general expectations as the "The Task of Management" and they are unique to the position of CFO of Newco Corp.

1. Contribute to the success and well-being of the executive team of Newco Corp by active, knowledgeable participation in general management discussions and policy making decisions.

2. Positively support executive teammates through education and knowledge sharing, constructive criticism, respect for time and experience, personal on-time contribution to departmental and general projects, celebration and recognition of victories, large or small, and concern for the development of the careers of your teammates.

3. Maintain financial reporting by degree, assuring that we are in compliance with federal and state tax law and reporting, as well as creating reporting metrics for our sales and operating teams that are simple, direct and well-communicated.

4. Remain current with professional trends in management, leadership and financial skills and convey those skills and experience to the Newco team.

5. Establish ongoing strategic plans that address the overall health and well-being of the organization. These plans should ensure that the company is prepared to deal with changes and quickly respond to the financial and operating challenges of the day.

6. Pay close attention to the detail of your department; meet regularly with your peers, administrative staff, controllers and general managers to ensure that direction, focus, and communication remain on "high alert" throughout the year and that the team is working synergistically.

7. Ensure that financial calls and meetings discuss your recommendations and finish with conclusions, directions and action plans. Ensure that these meetings are meaningful rather than a regurgitation of predictions that rarely are on target that offer us reason for loss but rarely reason or action to correct.

8. Be a leader in all situations by establishing clear and direct goals, monitoring progress against those goals and taking swift and decisive action in correcting any strategic miscues.

9. Develop your people, particularly those that have responsibility beyond their current knowledge and experience. Work closely to understand and appreciate the pressures and challenges faced by our sales team. Help them to find solutions that meet market demands and corporate objectives, and always seek to provide support rather than criticism. Areas most evidently in need are

international operations, and sales reporting in general.

10. Establish and maintain the highest level client, vendor, trade and industry relationships that can be relied upon to ensure the long-term health and well-being of the organization. These relationships should be viewed as solution and resource assets to you as an individual and to the company as a whole.

11. Plan opportunities to demonstrate your integrity and your commitment to the general health of the organization, even when it is not in the best interest of your immediate politics.

12. Review purchasing annually with all vendors with a consolidated spend of more than $10,000 seeking reductions and additional contributions to EBITDA.

13. Be prepared. Read all your communications thoroughly and be responsive to inquiries and proactive in your positions when you feel you may be asked questions. Think proactively about the perception you wish others to have about you and your department and be sure you are acting in a manner that ensures the success of that perception.

14. Pay attention to your IT responsibilities and make yourself an active partner with them. Understand that when IT falls behind, your organization falls behind and loss of creditability ensues. Build relationships with them and understand how they think, not just what they are trying to accomplish.

15. Be decisive and be a leader. Pointing out problems makes you a critic; pointing out solutions makes a leader, no matter your title or level of authority. Offer higher direction in difficult

times or difficult circumstances and be sure that your direction is contemporary to market demands and that you are reasonable in your judgment.

16. Have fun and make your work environment fun. Be a leader in making things fun and exciting. Be passionate about what you do and convey that passion to your team. Remember, a team of lambs led by a lion becomes lionlike; conversely, a team of lions led by a lamb become lambs. Be the Lion.

Mr. Joe Smith, Chief Financial Officer
Newco Corp

Objectives of Management 2019 (MBOs)

1. Consolidated Company EBITDA performance of a minimum of $16.9 million

Contribution: 25 percent of Earned "At-Risk" Compensation

Technical Metric: Consolidated 2019 Profit and Loss Statement

There is no middle ground in MBO #1 and no percentages paid out for performance below 100 percent of the $16.9 million.

2. GAAP Compliant Financial Reporting

Contribution: 25 percent of Earned "At-Risk" Compensation

Technical Metric: P&L and Balance Sheet Recast

Timeline: Ongoing with Calendar Quarterly Review

This MBO is to address the following categories and should include but not be limited to the following:

• Weekly, monthly, and annual financial reporting separating operational and financial metrics with concise recommendations

• All reports must follow GAAP standards

• Standardize transfer fees for cleaner, predictable and transparent cost accounting

• Summation report by division that follows P&L GAAP standards

• Expense consolidation to meet GAAP standards

• Install Inventory Management System

• Report and Advise on monthly sales report

• Weekly money management report in summation

• Bottom up budget process for fiscal 2020

• Reframed board book incorporating the above changes

3. Inventory Enterprise Solution On Track and On Time

Contribution: 25 percent of Earned "At-Risk" Compensation

Technical Metric: Implementation of Rev 200, twenty hours of enterprise training completed by all administration and sales personnel.

Timeline: July 1, 2019

IT Solution Inclusive of but not limited to:

• Inventory management

• Cost/pricing metric by account, division, region and sales professional

• Price index that is simple, online and restrictive by tier (product cannot be entered for sale if pricing is not within established perimeters)

• On target and on time 2019 IT budget

• Creation of IT deliverable list reviewed with executive staff monthly commencing 3.15.19

4. Complete Executive Emersion Program

Contribution: 25 percent of Earned "At-Risk" Compensation

Technical Metric: Certificate of completion

Timeline: August 15, 2019

CHAPTER 8

The Sales Conundrum

Right out of the gate I suggest that anyone who has the intention of sitting in the chief executive's chair gain direct sales experience and direct sales management experience. In my opinion, which is based not only on my own direct experience but in my observations of hundreds of CEOs over the last twenty-five years, it is the single greatest skill a senior executive, specifically a chief executive, should possess in order to competently lead an organization.

Let me start by doing a bit of qualifying. I do not believe a senior executive needs to be a great sales person. In fact, you may be as lousy at it as I was. You do need to be unconsciously competent at managing the sales discipline for your sales team, a sales organization, or an individual sales professional, because in your career as a CEO, you will at some time be forced into every one of those positions. Not having intimate experience and skill with this specific discipline can lead directly to revenue loss which may be difficult to recover from, and a great CEO never puts revenue in jeopardy.

Note that I used the word "managing" rather than leading as an experience descriptor. I mean that you need to understand the nuts and bolts of the sales process, from where to find them to how to terminate them with minimal organizational or client effect on revenue performance. (I also mean everything in between those two situations as well.)

Second, a bit of qualifying about myself in a sales role and why I wasn't very good at it. As you might imagine, I am a bit too direct for 99.99 percent of all customers. When I present my product to an end user, say the purchasing agent for a major retail store, there are several dynamics in play that prevent my ability to be reasonable.

Out of the gate I would not be standing in front of anyone if I did not believe my people, my product, my process, my culture, and my company were not the very best money could buy. In addition, I know how hard the entire company works to keep costs down and quality up. I know that everyone who works for me cares deeply about the job they do and their contribution to the success of the company. I know that we spend hours and hours figuring out how to be the best partner we can be with our customers and I know we bend over backward to accommodate even the smallest request. I know that my sales professionals are relentless in assuring on time/on target delivery, even if they have to pull and pack a late order themselves. I know that at the smallest hint of a quality question we replace or refund with no questions asked and we immediately make it right, no matter what it costs. That is the kind of sales culture I have always demanded of any organization I have been associated with.

So my example is a bit dramatic, but 100 percent accurate.

I received a call from my vice president of sales that my presence was requested at a meeting with a large national retail chain with whom we had quality issues. Interesting to note was that a year earlier, this retailer had asked us to import a cheaper product to replace the American-made counterpart we had been supplying to them for a decade. They cited price as their only consideration and admitted that although the import was inferior, the public would not notice the difference. Thus we were able to keep their business, albeit at lower margins, utilizing an imported product in place of our own. All factors that I was 100 percent opposed to and only allowed the deal as an interim step to winning back the American-made product.

Over the course of the year, we had experienced numerous quality issues with their import partner of choice. We stepped in front of the quality issues and fought like crazy with the import supplier; all invisible to the retailer, that totaled more than half a million dollars. Some of the bad product had shipped directly to the retailer and thus they were now aware of the quality issue. Our solution, take the product back and refund their money, then fight it out with the importer. That was our job.

So now we were to be taken to the shed for a whipping on the quality issue, and I was prepared to take the beating in stride. Sometimes they want to make sure they make their point by having the boss be there in person for the beating.

The broker on the deal, my VP of sales and I gathered at the appropriate time in the lobby of the corporate headquarters. Keep in mind that we represented a multi-national organization with revenues north of $300 million; we were not slackers or beggars looking for a new relationship. They had called out the top two executives from our organization which rivaled their own in size and revenue.

After waiting for almost two hours, we were escorted through a metal detector and security, to an elevator that whisked us up to the appropriate floor where we were placed, by a guard in uniform, in a tiny office with a table for four and a clock. Nothing else. No screen for our PowerPoint, no white board, no flip chart. Nothing. At exactly two o'clock, two purchasing guys entered the room which forced our broker to stand for the meeting. Neither had so much as a pen in their pocket or paper to use it on. The lead purchasing agent says we have twenty minutes to "make our case" as they are considering switching the business to a competitor. "The business" was twenty-five million annually, the relationship a decade old and until we began importing a product at their request, using a provider of their choice, our quality had never been an issue. Not even one time in ten years.

We pitched and explained but at the end of the day, they were non-committal and clearly under-impressed. At exactly twenty minutes past the hour, they stood up, thanked us for coming, and walked out of the meeting. The guard walked us stoically back to the elevator and to the door. We were done.

You can attend all the sales meetings, read all the books, listen to all the motivational speakers, even walk across the burning embers, but nothing prepares you for the kind of treatment sales professionals receive every day just like that encounter. While I wanted to jump over the table, grab this idiot by the neck and shake him until he wet his pants, my VP of sales took it all in stride, went back to the drawing board, and worked like a madman to earn the business back. He never quit and he never said even one bad word about the account or the people we dealt with.

That's the difference between sales professionals and the rest of the world. It's why they can, in many cases, earn more than the executive side of management. My goal in every position I have ever had is to surround myself with the greatest sales talent money can buy and clear every roadblock the rest of the world wants to put in their way. Good CEOs want sales accountability, lots of tracking reports and the same level of accountability in sales as we demand in production and operations. Great CEOs want revenue and they understand that it doesn't come easy and they are thankful for every dollar these professionals drag out of the customers pocket and deposit in the company's account. Great CEOs work relentlessly to keep costs down, margins up, and new products and campaigns flowing all for the single purpose of clearing the roadblocks and the "sales prevention specialists" out of the way.

Driving revenue is what makes and wins the day and great CEOs get it.

While many executives look at sales as somewhat of an art, I have always considered it more of a science if it is managed correctly. While there are many models you can look at as a CEO, the trick here is to keep everything about sales simple and uncomplicated. When you see things start to get buggered up with paperwork and reporting, that's a sure sign you have a sales prevention specialist hidden somewhere in the bushes. (Many times they are hiding out and can be disguised as a sales manager or even as your VP of sales.)

For definition purposes, we are talking about organic exponential growth (EG) as opposed to a standard mantra of year-over-year 15 percent norm, or acquiring growth with an acquisition or merger. I am a big fan of the latter but it is not always as easy to accomplish as the organic side might be. Also keep focused on the fact that I am offering you advice on the CEO perspective of the discipline and not from the sales professional's side. Your job as the CEO is to ensure that the overarching structure of the sales discipline is rock solid. Here are some foundational pillars that you are directly responsible for:

1. Is my product or service relevant, contemporary, and necessary to the consumption community for which it was designed to serve?

This is one of the most important questions a CEO must constantly, as in everyday, look in the mirror and be able to answer without bias, in the affirmative. So the story goes that you can lie to everyone else but you cannot lie to yourself when it comes to product/service viability. All products have a useful life and almost nothing lasts a lifetime so insuring that your offering is constantly updated, refreshed, and relevant is directly your responsibility. The minute you fall in love with your offering as is will be the day you begin your death spiral. That's one reason why great CEOs are always a bit on edge, never seem satisfied, and are always pushing for more. They know that the clock never stops ticking and they know that every day, on some level, they are fighting for their lives.

2. Is my product or service price-to-value proposition close enough for the consumption community market share I am asking for?

Once again, this takes some serious soul searching for you when you look in the mirror because you can demand all the growth you want from your sales division but if your answer to this question is not a resounding "yes" and your opinion vetted in spades by constant market surveys, you have a challenge. While we have all been to the myriad number of sales training seminars that denounce the horrible excuse of price as an excuse not to buy, you're living in the dark ages and wearing the "emperor's new clothes" if you think everything is not about price. That does not mean that people don't buy expensive things over cheap things. It does not mean that people don't buy from friends or from people they like over people they don't like, and it certainly does not mean that people will not pay a premium for the same product. It means simply that no matter where they buy their products and services, it always comes down to price. Period. They either can afford to pay the price or they can't. They might be able to pay the price but won't, or they might not do either. The question to ask here is: Are there enough consumers out there who both can and will pay my price, out of the entire consumption community, to support the market share I want?

3. Is my geography adequately covered?

This is a pretty simple question yet never ceases to amaze me when companies leave major parts of their intended geography uncovered and unprotected by a sales professional. Typically, we pay a lot of attention to communities directly around our home city, or state or region and then things seem to break down the farther out we go. While we all understand and expect that there are cultural differences when we travel abroad, we don't often take the impact of regional and local culture as seriously here in the United States. Whether your sales culture is supported internally, online, or with field sales professionals, local differences in buying patterns, price-to-value propositions and even product or service uses can be dramatically different. When we have realistic growth goals, supported by realistic geographic coverage, our chances for reaching new buyers exponentially increases.

4. Is my customer relationship management (CRM) system providing my sales professionals with the information they need to increase sales?

Let me translate this question into something a bit more field worthy. Is your CRM lightning fast, up to the second with account information on orders, deliveries, inquiries, pricing, historical information, contact information, email, and outstanding proposals on both active, inactive and prospect accounts? Do your sales professionals have field computers and do they know how to use your CRM on the fly?

In today's technological environment, you have to be able to answer this question with a resounding yes. I will make some really bold statements about sales professionals and I'm about to make my first one. Sales professionals do this job for two reasons: first, they hate oversight of any kind because they would rather work what they perceive as smart rather than hard; second, they are in it for the money and will not tolerate anything that gets in the way of that goal. This means lots of paperwork, reports, forms, ride-alongs, meetings, lack of internal support, internal people that they believe are slow, don't get it or don't do exactly what they ask them to do even if their request is unrealistic. On top of that, they want it done right now even if it means bumping another sales professional's request because at the end of the day, "it's all about me." As a CEO, you can either fight this ideology or you can understand it and support it. This does not mean that you tolerate poor or abusive behavior. What it does mean is that you understand that when a sales professional is fighting to get something done, or to not do something (paperwork), it's because they are fighting to keep a customer happy because for them, that gets them to their reasons for doing the job to start with.

5. Is my sales compensation plan, including base salary, bonus compensation, performance incentives, perquisites, and expense accounts relevant and contemporary? Are they sending the right message and motivating my sales professionals to perform to the goals and expectations of the company?

First understand that there are no perfect compensation plans for sales professionals. (Just ask yours and they will tell you all the mistakes you've made.) What's important to sales professionals is consistency rather than perfection. Once they figure it out, which means gaining ground on your program, they don't like a whole lot of change. I encourage you to be realistic. What if someone wanted to change your compensation plan and you didn't know how much you were actually going to make each week? Once again, you have to be contemporary and relevant with your sales compensation plan, while in addition, making slight changes that consistently motivate your sales professionals to move in the direction you want them to go.

6. Do I have a completely synergistic relationship between my sales professionals and the internal customer service team that supports them?

I have stopped counting the number of times I have been called into a business because "sales" was not performing to the expectations of management. One of the first things I look at is the relationship between customer service and the field sales professional. In many cases, the lack of performance is directly linked to a dysfunctional relationship between these two dynamic forces and it is something that as the CEO, you need to understand at a granular level. Great organizations engender a close and positive relationship between these two most important customer facing positions. By encouraging clear communication, a mutual understanding of needs, and the desire to work as a team in resolving customer challenges as well as collectively supporting additional opportunities to grow existing accounts, you will create world class service.

If you answered "no" to any of the above, it will be difficult to gain exponential growth (EG) which is what this book is all about so I am going to assume you're with me. This means that your product is relevant, priced right, market share available, your geography covered and your sales professionals supported with up to date information and technology; all prerequisites for achieving EG. I am also making some ginormous assumptions, such as from a global perspective, the company is poised to support EG. I only make this statement because nothing harms your reputation or your P&L more than taking off on an EG initiative and failing to deliver on product or service.

My life example of this happened early in my career when, as a young consultant, I was hired by the CEO of a tech company to design and implement a marketing campaign for a new cellular device. I was very excited, up for the challenge, and went to work. In the process of conducting my due diligence, I discovered that this product was so new that the engineer in charge of the product line was not sure of the cost or time of installation and he adequately warned me in my interview. I immediately went back to the CEO with my concern only to be told that this engineer always was negative and skeptical and that I should do the job for which he was paying me to do. He had made a large investment in this product and he wanted results right now. Off I went.

Two weeks after the implementation of my campaign, the company was backlogged in installation more than three months and it almost stalled in its tracks. Customers were upset, the product didn't work exceptionally well, it took three times as long to install as was initially projected and it greatly affected the general business of the company. The good news was I delivered a great campaign; the bad news was it could have put them out of business. Mental note to send the engineer some cookies.

Everything I mentioned in the previous paragraph is the direct responsibility of the chief executive officer; strategic, visionary and necessary in order to present this as a goal to your C-suite executives. The answer to every question is completely under your direct authority and responsibility to correct or endorse for acceptance, as should be the budget to support the EG initiative.

While I can set the stage for beginning the journey to EG in a few pages, do not let the enormity of the task of preparation go unnoticed. In some cases it has taken me years to stage a company for EG from literally every perspective. The change in cultural attitude, the belief factor enjoyed by senior sales executives who have never been challenged with EG in their careers, the monumental task of preparing operations for this kind of growth can be extremely challenging to an organization at multiple levels. My experience is that the CEO must lead this charge herself and be visible and available for consultation throughout the process. In some cases, it requires the loosening of "protected territory" that your clients have enjoyed for years, or perhaps a change in your distributor agreements. It may mean that your sales professionals who enjoyed huge geography for years, now find themselves splitting up these gold mines to share with newbies. As much as you see possibilities, you will run into challenges that affect your people at every juncture and in many cases, the only assurance that things will be all right will come from your mouth. Good luck with that.

CHAPTER 9

The Secret to Positive IT/ Enterprise Implementation: Leadership

If you were a C-suite executive in the 1990s like I was, you no doubt were part of the enterprise explosion that rocked the business world for the entire decade. We learned a lot in those years about how fast the world of information technology was moving and at that time, it was not simply a question of selecting off-the-shelf software and installing it in the cloud. As a CEO, IT represented a significant investment in organizational infrastructure that affected everything from the physical space necessary to house your hardware, to the HVAC systems that managed the environment necessary to operate these massive banks of machines.

I remember in the late 1990s spending the majority of my time working daily with my VP of IT designing our hardware infrastructure to support our new enterprise system. Once that laborious process was complete, we spent the better part of a year going through a very painful and costly software implementation that upset every aspect of our standard operation procedures, as well as putting significant burden on our culture, as painful and disruptive changes made every day a challenge.

Fast forward to 2014 and I find myself sitting in a business forum with a dozen young CEOs meeting up to discuss challenges and obstacles they are facing as they build their businesses and it sounds like 1998 all over again. One CEO challenges the room with a question on how to get his people to accept the changes they need to make in order to fully utilize the new enterprise system he has spent hundreds of thousands of dollars on. His board is upset as the implementation is taking too long and they are losing competitive advantage without it. His sentiments are echoed around the room as one of his colleagues also throws down on the inability of his IT people to be effective in managing the process through. Should he invest in hardware infrastructure? Should he go to the cloud? Will he lose his firewalls if he moves out of his own operating environment? His IT people are offering him information but not decisions, leaving him scouring the Internet for solutions. He's angry and losing faith in his IT chief.

These sentiments are not unusual as the space of IT continues to reshape itself in months rather than years, and sometimes even days can make a difference in how this space looks and operates. Looking at cellular use alone, we see new operating platforms emerge to the masses every few months that completely change the way we communicate. Since our handhelds now support the same data that used to be available only on highly sophisticated land-locked hardware, we must continually change our approach to managing our IT processes.

Here are a handful of tips that will take away some of the pain you may be experiencing in your approach to IT development.

1. If you're not IT savvy, it's time to learn. I want to distinguish here the difference between knowing how to use your smartphone for getting e-mail, and being IT savvy. IT savvy means that you have and maintain at least a rudimentary understanding of system architecture; that is, how your system works and what it works on. Capacity and the ability to grow to meet the needs of the future lies directly in your hands and this information must be within your grasp in order for you to effectively manage organizational strategy. There are many colleges and universities that offer immersion courses for executives that last five to ten days and will give you the knowledge you need to keep up, direct, and ask the right questions of your IT staff to get the information you need.

2. IT reports directly to the CEO. If you're one of those CEOs who has IT reporting through your CFO, or worse, through your COO, you need to change that structure today. The days of IT taking a back seat to other executive management positions are over and you need to have that direct contact and direct management over this most important piece of your infrastructure. My experience is that IT executives are different folks: they think differently, they often act differently, and many times they do not fit in with the stereotypical norm of your other direct reports. The technical language they speak often needs some interpretation and some supervision in order for the message to be understood. Get over it, and help the rest of your staff get over it as well. These professionals need a voice at the table and you need their ears at the table. A great IT executive can listen and relate systems performance or systems needs to what she is hearing at the executive staff meeting and can translate those challenges into solutions.

3. Become a dynamic leader of change. This is easier said than done, but don't lose the message. While everyone wants and often demands change, put a new operating system in front of Bill and tell him his production reports are not going to look like they used to and watch Bill's blood pressure immediately blow off the charts. Your job as a CEO is to proactively acknowledge the pain change brings to people who do the same task-related data oversight every day. By telling people what to expect, why it is important, and how they will be supported through the process will give you a much needed leg up on those detractors who will hate the new system no matter what you do. Rewarding and encouraging those team mates most affected will pay you incredible dividends on your way to systems utilization and integration. As a CEO, you need to be knowledgeable, empathetic, and visible when your people are feeling the pain of change.

4. Manage the deliverables as opposed to managing the project. Leaders often feel that if this thing is going to go right, they need to manage the details. Do not give in to that ideology when you're championing enterprise implementation.

Rather, learn to manage the deliverables, the timelines, and the key milestones, but not the process, and never get involved with managing the consultants or vendors on the project; always make them follow through with your IT chief. My experience is that these people will bother you incessantly with the smallest details rather than deal with a demanding, knowledgeable IT chief. Let everyone know on the front end, that missing deadlines and rising costs will not be tolerated.

5. Be a realist but don't be taken advantage of. My experience, on more than a dozen major software enterprise projects costing millions of dollars is that it costs twice as much in both dollars and time as you originally were advised. It doesn't have to be this way if you are diligent on the front end with vendor scrutiny, consultant support, and managing assumptions into reasonable timelines and deliverables. Once in place, be a fierce leader when it comes to meeting objectives and be a demanding leader when it comes to vendors living up to their end of the agreements, both documented and implied. If at any time you are unhappy with the support from vendors or consultants, immediately resolve the issue by moving up the hierarchy of their organization. Let your people know that you will hold suppliers to the same level of scrutiny and professionalism that you hold them to.

6. Be the heart and the fist of customization. You will be pressured to customize the new system to make it right for your operations. Rather than immediately give in to those recommendations, take a 360 degree look and see if your business might operate more effectively or at least as effectively if you changed your standard operating procedures to match the system design. You do this for several reasons: first, customization always costs a bundle and that's bad. But more significantly, future upgrades will always cost more and have more problems in implementation than the original design, because someone has to remember to lay them over the upgrade. Trust me, it is a fool's errand. You never know what idiosyncrasy is going to mess up your system when customization runs smack dab into revision number 200. Instead, make general recommendations to your software writer and urge them to incorporate your suggestions into future versions of the basic system. This is much cheaper and the burden of change and development falls to the provider and not to you. When customization is necessary, be sure your staff keeps better than adequate records on its recommendations so that you don't wind up doing things two, three, and four times over again.

On a side note, it took me several times of allowing too much of what I call "system bastardization" before I realized that sometimes your own staff can take you down the road of discord. On one occasion, we actually lost the value of much of what we paid for and initially loved about our new system when one employee refused to go along with a new look to her beloved sales reports. By the time she was done ordering redesign and custom written change orders, our new system looked just like our old system and we gained absolutely nothing after spending more than a $100,000. She was very happy that she didn't have to learn anything new and we were still so reliant on her custom software, she dictated the terms of her employment. Not for long, but the price of change is sometimes not as evident as you might think.

When I first started out, like most other CEOs, I had the IT chief and her team reporting to my CFO. This accomplished two things; the CFO had every report he or his staff could think of, and the rest of us continued to wait to gain sales and operating information we felt we desperately needed. Second, the IT world was a black hole that, like finance, was always a bit behind the organization in meeting objectives. There was always a waiting line of folks trying to get information that never seemed to diminish no matter how many consultants or overtime hours we paid for.

In 1996, we had decided to bite the bullet and go for a new operating system that included a complete connection from order entry through operations and culminating in new financial reporting. It was a massive project that was scheduled to take us a year (dream on), and about $500,000 in capital (dream on again), as well as taking an enormous amount of in-house employee time. When we were about six months into the project, things were already off track and heading south in a hurry. I couldn't get answers out of my CFO (in charge of project), my IT guy was ready to jump off the bridge, and the organization was coming quickly to a standstill.

The event that was to force a change was a conversation with my CFO, a very bright young woman who was a star as a CFO but, I realized, knew less about IT than I did at the time. I changed the reporting structure and had the IT chief report directly to me. In our first meeting he outlined his concerns and ideas to resolve the challenges but clearly trying to work these ideas through the CFO wasn't gaining us any ground. The decisions this young guy was trying to make were way above his pay grade and as most of them required decisions on spending what it took to be successful, the CFO had quite naturally nixed them all as they were not part of her annual budget and more to the point, not part of the initial bid for the project. The CFO was making decisions based on her sandbox of authority when we were drowning in a dry pool. This was a major turning point in my career as I realized that IT was becoming an animal of a different color and it required me to become educated and aware of the emerging technology world. I went back to school, read everything I could get my hands on, and became at least marginally capable of getting us through the implementation.

This is just one of a thousand reasons why, as a CEO, you must continue to evolve, to grow to not only improve yourself, but to be capable of leading change in others.

These are some keys to finding solid IT executives that are worth sharing and may save you the time of discovering them yourself.

Cast a wide net. As I have said before, cast your net wider than you might normally think necessary in order to have a variety of folks to talk to.

Hands off the software suppliers. I have not found it advantageous to hire the talent away from my lead software supplier, no matter how much your staff likes him.

There are two important questions to ask potential candidates. First, "How many enterprise implementations have you managed?" (not participated in, managed.) Good follow up questions are constructed around talking through how they managed them. Second, "Do you embrace your architecture sitting in-house or in the cloud?" Good follow ups are constructed around the "whys." If you hear a lot of protectionism around keeping things in-house and/or an inbred philosophy of cloud distrust, it may offer insight into how your future IT capital cost may be affected by the candidate. While keeping machines and dark pipe in-house may be your methodology of choice, it is quickly becoming difficult to afford the luxury of real estate and maintenance of complex hardware.

Do not be afraid of hiring talent that may seem overqualified for the job. There are many seasoned IT chiefs who, once they finish major projects, are simply ready for a new environment. My experience is that IT people get bored very quickly when the company moves into maintenance mode.

The best IT executives I have worked with are the kind of people who are not afraid to step out and help you lead organizational change. When you are comfortable with your IT talent, you're not afraid to let them do just that. The world of technology is still out in front of us and as leaders, we have to recognize what's out there, and figure out how to use it to competitive advantage.

CHAPTER 10

Growth

It's always interesting to me when, wearing my consultant's hat, I sit down with a CEO who is setting up her annual strategic planning session for her executive staff and the question of growth is raised. In the tee-up for facilitating these sessions, I need to know how much leeway the CEO is going to offer her staff in deciding how the company will operate, as opposed to her laying out the goals and leaving the team to decide how to get there.

When I bring up growth, 90 percent of the time I already know the answer I'm going to hear: "Fifteen percent year over year" is the answer of choice. When I probe as to why 15 percent, the follow-up is also pretty much burned into the turf: "Well, I think that's about what the team can expect to do."

When you take on the task of running an organization, you have to look at a lot of different factors in understanding what the job will really entail relative to its consistency and sustainability. Even when discussing expectations with board chairs or directors, I have never received much direction on the growth question, which leaves it up to you to do some homework. One of the big lessons here is before you take on the task, you need to get your hands on some financial statements to fully understand what you're getting in to. Short of the company providing full disclosure, you at least need gross revenue and earnings before interest, taxes, depreciation and amortization (EBITDA) numbers for the past three to five years before agreeing to go to work. In reviewing this information, you can see growth expectations, anomalies in financial performance, and the trend lines on a forward look. This information is paramount to your truly understanding the approach to operating this business in the top seat.

Here is an example of how things can get a bit sideways in this process.

In the late 1990s I was approached to take over an organization that was privately owned by a family who had no immediate involvement with the day-to-day business operations. The family held two board seats out of seven but allowed this company to operate as its own entity, similar to a public held entity with the exception that any derived profits rolled over into the family trust. The grandfather, who had founded the organization, had passed away the prior year, although he had been retired from the business for several years. I was to replace the current CEO who was also retiring after a long career with the organization in a number of key rolls.

In researching both the industry and the company, I found that the industry was not the barn burner that it had been back in the day, although the business itself was clearly the industry leader. Technology was quickly taking over the industry and I was having a hard time picturing the need for its product and services in the years ahead, so the future was in question. That being said, even those businesses that have become extinct by changing technology can sometimes find a niche if they are playing at the top of their industry, and in this case, that was a possibility. The "last man standing" philosophy has been played out successfully in many cases in spite of the great technological evolution that has claimed so many industries.

In my interviews with the board, there was definitely a feeling that this company was poised to grow and the directors were tossing out some relatively big numbers. They claimed to have the war chest to fuel significant growth and were looking for an aggressive leader to take them there. Man, this was right on the money for me. I started to get really excited about the possibility of cleaning house on the competition and if the industry was shrinking, taking all the market share I could as fast as possible. I also began to daydream about what other opportunities the company might look at if the primary product was becoming antiquated. With a big war chest to invest, there was no telling what we might do.

I was having lunch with the company's bankers a week into this process and while doing my job of selling my capabilities, I was interviewing them as well, searching for the historical look-back from the bank's perspective. They seemed a bit more reserved than the board when the discussion turned to investment opportunities with the war chest. It turned out that the company had been struggling through the last few years as the market continued to deteriorate and losses over the past two years had reflected this trend quite heartily. The single bright spot, as the bankers saw it, was that when the grandfather/founder passed away, his key man policy kicked in to the tune of $7 million dollars which was the only contributor to the company's well-being in the past five years and the only way the company was able to clean up its breach of bank covenants. I was gone in sixty seconds. The company did wind up finding a very qualified guy to take on the task, but by the time he really got a handle on it, it was time to shut the lights off and divvy up the last of the leftover cash.

There are many benefits to reviewing financial statements of prospective employers that go way beyond the gross and net numbers. I have often found that organizations, especially those that are aged a bit, tend to crash operational numbers into the pure financial performance documents. While the operating team might understand the relativity of the association, if a company doesn't practice generally accepted accounting principles (GAAP) it always makes me a tad nervous, in addition to making the audit firm crazy trying to straighten out the annual audit numbers. But it shows you very clearly what the company values in terms of performance. I have found that the adage of "companies measure what they care about" to be by far one of the truest idioms of business.

Another practice which I strongly encourage, is to be sure that the income statement carries a column for the percentage of expense to gross revenue ratios. This to me is the fastest way to spot a number of anomalies both on a year to year basis as well as the fastest way to see which expenses are out of normal, either for you as the leader coming in to a new situation, for the industry as a whole, or for the organization you're interested in. In many businesses, while one particular ratio may appear out of the normal range for you, it may be perfectly normal for the industry. An example might be an organization that co-ops marketing and advertising with its clients and records this as a discount on the invoice rather than recording the cost as a direct marketing expense. The income statement would not accurately reflect the advertising expense to gross ratio, but it would not necessarily change the financial performance of the company.

Once you have an understanding of the financial performance and the board's goals clearly in hand, it's time to roll up your sleeves and do what you do best. (This is also where the fun starts.)

No matter your defined strategic growth direction—organic, merger, acquisition, new products/services or perhaps model changes—there is one thing that you can never forget as a CEO. Growth requires people to change some of their most valued beliefs, attitudes, behaviors, and activities and that, my friends, is the rub. Great CEOs, who are also great growth leaders, never forget this, and those CEOs who can manage change, manage people through change, eliminate the inevitable roadblocks and actively engage the organization are worth their weight in gold.

I have never been much of a maintenance guy when it comes to taking on leadership engagements; to me there is not a lot of fun in a game where no one is trying to increase the numbers on the scoreboard. Many leaders will suffer along with the 15 percent numbers for years and years without ever thinking about 30 percent, 50 percent, or even 100 percent year to year growth, or about challenging the status quo outside of organizational "normal." I have found over the years that just getting a team to think like that is a huge challenge for most organizations.

These six ways to exponentially increase organically generated gross revenue were outlined and defined in chapter eight on sales, and are recapped here for emphasis. Worth indelibly etching them in your mind, I tend to take them on in this order:

1. **Valid and Contemporary Product or Service**

   Is our product or service relevant and contemporary? Are we not only a reasonable solution but the best solution for our market?

2. **Solid Price to Value Proposition**

   Does our consumption community accept our price as reasonable for the product, service, or task we are providing?

3. **Geography and Market Coverage**

   Are we adequately covering, growing and protecting both the geography we serve and the consumption community within those perimeters?

4. **Does our enterprise and customer management software support our growth mission?**

   Are we able to use our systems as a strategic advantage? Can we instantly provide information that supports our current clients?

5. **Sales Compensation and Incentive Programs**

   Are we contemporary in our sales compensation plan, and are we motivating our sales professionals toward the appropriate goals?

6. Internal Support

Do we understand and support our sales professionals and our clients through outstanding communication and instant information? Do we understand that if we are not talking directly to a customer we should be supporting those that do with 110 percent effort?

Digging deep into these six areas of your business will pay you growth dividends every time. Believe everything people tell you and then vet everything they say. Opinions are wonderful and they typically carry one or two anecdotal stories that support a belief; but vetting for hard numbers cannot be substituted when it comes to effecting growth. Many organizations do not measure the functional deliverables of these areas below a cursory level. In order to exponentially increase sales, you have to be hitting these pitches out of the park.

Along the path of discovery, you will find that it quickly becomes evident who the "sales prevention specialists" in the organization are, and I promise you will often be surprised at the titles they hold. In my thirty years, I have seen more senior executives such as the vice president of sales, the chief financial officer, and even the vice president of human resources who could have been classified with that title. Once people believe there is a wall between what they have and what they want, many folks will not only stop when they hit it, they will work very hard to be sure others stay far away from it.

Here is one example that made me absolutely crazy when I was first starting out.

In looking through the process I outlined above, it became

really evident that the company I was working with had really poor geographic coverage: more than half the United States was covered by one senior sales professional who was a lot closer to retirement than to career development, if you get my drift. The company simply didn't speak to its customers on a regular basis. The sales guy had long tenure with the organization and the numbers he produced were out of this world. Of course they were. He covered the world and tolerated not one intrusion into his territory. He had stopped traveling several years before, and made the majority of his sales on the telephone. Everyone in the organization protected him due to his tenure, and even the C-suite was afraid to disturb this gentlemen as he constantly threatened to quit, take his business with him, and ruin the organization. He, like many other sales professionals I've met over the years, was holding the company hostage. At that moment, I made a promise never to negotiate with kidnappers or sales prevention specialists.

Much to the angst of everyone in the executive suite, I called this sales rep to my office. (It was amazing how many executives had appointments outside of the office that day including the VP of sales, who the guy reported to.) Initially, I got the same threats and self-important bullshit that this guy typically won his arguments with. I waited, not patiently, for him to get it all off his chest which took considerable time. I even gave him the opportunity to catch his breath several times so he could keep going. He finally threw out the threat he always did about quitting, and I just as quickly accepted his resignation. He almost fell on the floor when I asked for his keys. After turning several shades of purple, we were able to have a nice chat about how things would be going forward. We split his territory and accounts four ways, we helped ease him into a different compensation arrangement over a period of time, and we began to reach out to customers and build the business beyond what they could have imagined if left to their old ways.

This makes it sound relatively easy and without any real problems when, in fact, it is anything but easy, and full of potential pitfalls. Around this one issue, we had to change the entire sales compensation plan, hire and train new sales professionals, reconnect with our clients, increase our travel and expense costs, and on top of all of this, we had to document the detail of every conversation we had with our problem guy so that if he came back on us later, claiming discrimination or a hostile work environment, we could defend ourselves reasonably. To complicate matters, I very quickly became persona non grata to all of the senior sales professionals and many of the executives who were longtime friends with my problem guy. They figured I just as easily could have fired them, or worse, keep them around with diminished titles and lower compensation. They thought I screwed the guy.

Several years down the road, when we had increased sales by almost 30 percent, had a great new group of sales professionals with happy clients and increased profits, our annual strategic planning facilitator asked why we were in that position at our annual planning session. After several minutes of deliberation in groups, the VP of sales stood up and said something about how he learned through a leadership meeting how important this was and, although difficult, he was paid to make the tough decisions.

I almost fell out of my chair. But if you're thinking you're ever going to get a thank you or a pat on the back when you're a CEO, dream on. I changed the history and culture of that organization and didn't even get recognized as a contributor to the process.

THE IMPORTANCE OF PAD

One area that is very often overlooked in the growth initiative analysis is the necessary attention to ongoing product application and development (PAD). I like to see a PAD team that is watching the current numbers closely while staying significantly ahead of the market. In many cases, senior executives don't see the necessity in an ongoing PAD spend and oftentimes relegate the function to a backroom engineer. When the shit hits the fan and customer needs or requirements change, or worse, a competitor successfully mimics us, we then expect to catch up with Mr. Market in short order, typically with poor results. Rushing products to market to maintain market share and gross revenue is probably one of the largest contributors to a business entering a death spiral. That being said, the market today has a habit of releasing technology (AKA "Apps") early and then downloading fixes that allow customers to sort out the bugs. Keep in mind that this is not a mistake, but rather a planned strategy to increase "to market" speed while keeping engineering costs down. Try this with a new titanium knee replacement and you likely will not have the same results.

Once you have looked at the analysis of these questions and vetted the information, it should become relatively apparent where you need to invest in order to grow the organization. Typically this means something or someone has to change, and that's where the pain factor dramatically increases and the excitement that was there at your arrival begins to diminish a bit. When that apex crosses lines, it is extremely important that you are visible and overcommunicating with your team and the organization. This is not a time to allow staff to carry your message; you need to be front and center, doing that yourself. With change comes uncertainty, and communicating reassurance that you have the skill, experience and education necessary to successfully guide the company through the challenge is of paramount value.

While there are many challenges to accomplishing growth change, there are two things you can do that I have found work really well.

First, operate with the spirit of inclusion and participation. While I'm not encouraging your workplace be a democracy, I do encourage the team to be deeply involved in both process and decision making. If you do your job right, they will come to the conclusion you want them to without forcing them into it, and this in turn makes them advocates of change and challenge.

Second, before you open the checkbook and take off on a growth journey, make sure in every respect that your organization is ready to grow. IT systems, supply chain, CRM, training, production, supply; there is no area that goes untouched when you're looking for exponential increases and a stutter start here can wreak havoc on an organization that will take years to unravel.

MERGER AND/OR ACQUISITIONS

While I am a firm believer in continuous organic growth, there are times when acquiring a competitor can make a lot of sense. For many organizations and even for many CEOs, the world of mergers and acquisitions can be a bit daunting and complex. In many cases, competitors who you have been battling with for years become the most likely candidates for acquisition and that can be both difficult and problematic for organizational culture. I have been personally involved with more than forty transactions; some of them easy and executed on the back of a napkin over breakfast, others complex and full of regulation and legal haranguing. I am proud of the fact that while not every deal turned out wonderfully well, I have not ever faced any legal action as a result of such a transaction.

Like any new process or concept a new CEO might bring into an organization, acquiring for growth should be a process that is understood, trained into the executive suite, and ingrained into the culture prior to any actual attempts to engage. If an organization has little or no history with growing in such a manner, priming the pump will pay you big dividends down the road.

I was working with a relatively stagnant organization as a consultant and, as in most cases, was pointing out the obvious ways and means to growth. The executive team was young and full of energy while the CEO was older and just didn't want to put the energy into any changes in thinking. He was very content to maintain the status quo and retire gracefully. I was trying to walk the fine line between making my client, the CEO, happy, while at the same time asking questions that were thought provoking in hope of having a participant engage in the various new ways to increase revenue.

So, it was with less than stellar enthusiasm that as I pushed the group to raising the question of acquiring growth, the CEO grudgingly agreed that while there may be some validity to that course of action, it was best if the team concentrated on what they knew how to do organically. He felt that once they had exhausted all of those options, they could look at acquisitions. Further, in his learned opinion, people who bought other companies ultimately failed (true by most statistics) at reaching their original goals for acquiring the competitor to begin with.

While that conversation stopped the talk of making acquisition a strategic initiative that year, the CEO did acquiesce to me, helping any interested members of the executive staff write a program and process for acquiring growth. Sometimes you lose the battle and win the war and ultimately that felt pretty good for everyone. Shortly after that session, we completed a project coded "Anaconda" which was a comprehensive guide to project managing an acquisition which is some of the best work I have ever initiated or been associated with. Five years after that project was completed, and two years after the CEO retired, the team put that project to use on an acquisition of their second largest competitor. Not only was the acquisition made, but the target integrated with enormous success and facilitated in record time. Every member of the executive team with the full knowledge and support of their respective operational teams was deeply involved in the integration, which resulted in 30 percent growth in gross revenue and ultimately a huge gain in efficiency which translated to increased profitability.

There are several points to take away here.

First, not everyone can be included in the initial negotiations. In fact, I strongly recommend that you as the CEO begin the negotiations by yourself. This usually means meeting one-on-one with your counterpart and talking in very general terms. What you're really looking for is understanding what the motivations are for selling, which is often more difficult to find out when you have a lot of people around. For some, they are just tired and want out. For others, they are trying to get out before they go bankrupt, and there is every other reason under the sun you can imagine and I've heard many. Once understood, I have always found that keeping that goal first and foremost in my mind makes me both empathetic towards helping another CEO achieve his objective. Also, more selfishly, it helps me in keeping things real when folks throw out crazy numbers. And they always do. Your job is to marry the objective with reality. Sometimes it works, and sometimes it doesn't. In the acquisition game, you always have to be able to walk away without a second thought. The minute you get emotionally involved and it becomes a win/lose, you've already lost. Conversely, if you are selling something, the minute you start spending the money while you're still negotiating the deal, I've already won.

The late, great Steven Covey, who offered the world his excellent Seven Habits of Highly Effective People, had an especially wonderful concept. He called it win/win or no deal. I have tried as hard as I could to keep that motto in everything

I have ever done. I have not always been successful at it, but I sure believe in it. If you can create a situation where everyone knows what the win is for both sides of the table, and you all work toward helping the other party hit theirs, it pays dividends beyond your imagination. The minute you start putting your win ahead of anyone else's win, more often than not it becomes a losing situation for everyone. I can say without a doubt that many of my mistakes can be directly attributed to those times when I lost focus on that one habit. When you start thinking that "It's good to be king," and that as CEO you get to do or say anything you want, that's when your ticket gets punched. And rightfully so.

Relative to the CEO facilitating the initial contact and gaining understanding of the motivation for sale, I expect that the CEO can bring a Conditional Letter of Intent to the table for review and consideration by her executive team. I expect her to be able to write conditional terms, get close to price and finance agreements, and outline any considerations beyond those terms that are of concern. Since it is a conditional LOI, the outcome is totally reliant on following a full due diligence disclosure process and review of all entity documents and proof of facts before the CLOI becomes binding as an LOI. The deal can then be shared with the executive team who should all have an interest and task in the due diligence process. Once your team is in the game, it's time to get counsel involved in reviewing the deal.

I always made it part of the process to bring less experienced executive team members into the due diligence process, often having them handle disciplines they were unfamiliar with. For example, if you want an analytic take on the target's sales performance, having your operating executive review the sales process and vet the numbers pays dividends in many ways. The COO can see production volumes, become familiar with product or service, review gross margins, etc. The list can go on and on but it becomes a great learning experience. As CEO, you can never abdicate your authority over the process, but you can delegate a task that allows for your executives to gain knowledge and experience that will help them in their career path.

In one case, I had several active deals moving at the same time and we were all forced to wear a lot of hats. During this period, every one of my C-suite executives had an opportunity to handle the legal aspect of a transaction. This experience would prove invaluable to their career development, and several of them were able to utilize this experience as they moved into the CEO chairs themselves. The only thing better than doing it yourself is to know you helped someone else develop the confidence to take on the task.

As most successful CEOs or turnaround CEOs will tell you, growth is addictive and like any other skill, must be paired with good judgment and reason. You have to know when your team is tapped out and be sure you are giving them the recovery time necessary to conduct their business and adjust after a growth spurt. In the M&A world, it's imperative that your team assimilates the business you gained and maintains superb relationships with your new customers, be they internal or external. Growth may also cause you to rethink your supply chain agreements, vendor sourcing, sales channels and a host of other things that take time to sort out. The key as you have read many times, is that the CEO must be up front and visible during these challenging times, filled with support, encouragement and lots of engagement with employees at every level.

CHAPTER 11

Strategy

You can read a lot of material on the importance of leadership and the impact of confidence in a team environment and mountains of books on how to make friends and influence people. Those are all wonderful and uplifting. If you want to grow a business, however, the following is what separates success and failure. Formed strategy and the ability to execute is the single biggest key to being successful as a chief executive officer, an owner, a turnaround gal or any other successful key leadership position. It will get you promoted; it will give your career a boost, no matter where you sit in the food chain, and without it, you're flailing like a drunken man at a piñata and you might get lucky, but you'll never get the prize.

The secret is organizational strategy. It's not phantom or random or obscure. It's not hard to get and it's not hard to see. A mediocre team can execute on it, a great team can exceed all expectations, and an exceptional team will take you to places you never thought you could go. So why doesn't everyone have this strategy, and why can't all organizations operate at exceptional levels?

There really are two simple answers to these questions, and both have to do with the CEO.

First, most CEOs don't spend enough time considering what's really important to growing and sustaining a viable enterprise. They get too caught up in protecting profits, protecting the status quo, protecting employees, protecting the bank covenants, protecting their customers, and protecting their own asses. Growth requires great forethought and, in many cases, great risk. Rarely have I met CEOs who are willing to risk everything to achieve extraordinary results, even when those risks are minimized by great talent, enough cash to fuel great opportunity, and the support of a great board encouraging you to go after extraordinary growth and opportunity.

Most CEOs espouse a belief in thinking and acting strategically, but many, in my experience, have no idea how to get it done or make it part of their culture. One key attribute of a great CEO is to understand that in order to be successful he must subjugate his ego and his natural tendency to control, in support of the best organizational outputs, as defined by the entire team of executives responsible for its success. Unfortunately, most CEOs I have worked with are unwilling to let go of that control and in most cases wind up driving goals that are broad in texture and therefore lack enough definition to get any traction. Many CEOs don't understand the difference between mission, vision, goals, strategic initiatives, and projects, and do not fully understand their connection as well as the differences between these key concepts. Again, my own experience is that many CEOs consider this process to be "fluff" and do not really understand how important these factors are in defining business culture. They don't want to spend a lot of time and certainly no money on such soft efforts. My opinion is that failure to define these five important success ingredients, failure to include any of these five factors, and failure to execute on any one of these factors and the organization will eventually fail to meet expectations.

Second, over the years I have become amazed at the number of CEOs who delegate this task of setting up and staging the annual planning retreat to HR, the CFO, or the VP of sales. In some cases they then choose not to participate directly, or conversely, get excited about a bunch of new ideas hanging from flip charts but never assign or delegate the authority or responsibility for follow up and follow through. I have had numerous CEOs complain about the team not accomplishing anything when in fact, it was his or her job to ensure that these great ideas were acted upon.

In my tenure as a CEO, I engaged a number of consultants from around the country to facilitate our strategic planning process and eventually learned a lot from these folks. Over the years, I might not have always been totally happy with a particular process or program, or thrilled with the facilitator, but I realized early that attempting to facilitate my own session was a terrible mistake. You just can't be objective with your own team and no matter how hard you try, you wind up dominating the program. Once your team feels that cloak, they withdraw and you don't get the benefit of free thinking. Eventually I would learn how to participate, when to participate, and when to get the hell out of Dodge. The first time I left a session with my team and the facilitator, I paced outside of the hotel for an hour wondering if I should go back in because there was one more thing I had to get out. Thankfully, I was smart enough to leave it alone and that breakthrough allowed my team to grow beyond me. The learning key here is to pay the money and hire outside professionals to facilitate your session and it will pay you dividends beyond your imagination.

I remember in the early 2000s talking with a good friend about his business which was service oriented and while he had muscled the business up to $20 million, he was losing interest with continually trying to grow and push his team to bigger numbers. Phil was a bit of a tough guy and was often tougher than he needed to be on his executives. He was also a real tightwad and wouldn't spend a nickel on anything but himself.

He was disillusioned with his work and his staff and he wanted me to help him tee up the business for sale. My first recommendation was that we get his team together for a strategy session and see how we could make this business look polished and attractive. He reluctantly agreed and fought with me over my fee until I shaved it down to nearly free. So much for friendship.

I brought Sharon in for the behavior part of the session and watched as she did her magic in getting the team talking and interacting in a really positive manner. These executives weren't disillusioned, and they were engaged and interested from the minute they walked in. Certainly they were a far cry from the incompetent and angry folks Phil had told me about. He was the one who was a bit sullen and withdrawn and it wasn't long before Sharon picked up on that and started to work him. It took her about an hour to get him to engage and lighten up a bit but slowly he began to pick his head up and he even laughed at himself a few times with the exercise Sharon had him engaged in.

Over the two and a half day session, we put that team to work in a big way. We argued, looked at numbers, went over some ideas and opportunities that his team had been looking at. We forced Phil to define some growth objectives that matched up with the concepts the team was delivering and we also forced him to be positive in his approach. He was reluctant the first day, engaged the second and by the end of the session, he had become a cheerleader for the strategic initiatives his team had collectively developed.

Over the course of the next year, we worked closely with Phil and his team executing on their strategy and making sure everything was moving. We didn't waste time on things that didn't work and concentrated efforts and capital on things that did. We analyzed our numbers and reported our successes and failures to every employee in the company. By the end of the year we had great traction and the company was alive at every level.

In a year-end wrap up meeting, I advised Phil that I was ready to pursue a suitor for his company and felt his multiple would be in the right range now. I thought he was going to punch me. He was out of his seat yelling that his business wasn't for sale and that he had the greatest team in the world and he was making more money than he ever had. Then he told me that my fees were too high and he was spending way too much money on consulting for me to get an idea like that in my head. Some things don't change. Sharon would wind up firing Phil as a client a year or two later when he pissed her off one too many times with his attitude. I just shook my head.

There are many ways to facilitate strategic planning within

your organization and there are some pitfalls to be aware of. As I mentioned, defining some terms is the first step, and making sure the entire team is on board with expectations is of paramount importance. In order to help you help yourself and make that contribution I talked about in the first paragraph, I'm going to lay out a planning map for you to follow. You may find that there are some timing issues specific to your business, so just make adjustments in the timelines to suit your needs and then look at the relative action to see if it works for you.

STRATEGIC PLANNING FORMULA AND TIMELINE

1. On a calendar year financial reporting system, June is an appropriate time for the CEO to begin to stage the annual strategic planning process (SPP). The following tasks are the responsibility of the CEO.

- Identify and contract with the SPP facilitator. This includes a face-to-face meeting to discuss the program, program goals, costs, and expectations. Recommended target date for this off-site meeting would be early September.
- Meet with executive admin to select venue, budget, attendees, and materials. Executive admin will then book venue, arrange food and lodging, examine travel needs of attendees, etc.
- Meet with attendees, offer information on a need to know basis such as save the date and any special considerations. This is not a time to offer too much information as things may change between now and your planning session.

- This is an appropriate time to begin to measure any metrics you might have your eye on relative to challenges or opportunities.

- Begin to frame organizational near- and long-term goals; discuss goals with facilitators for clarity and presentation.

2. In June, begin to meet (once a week) separately with what I call the "Big 5": CEO, COO, CFO, VP/HR, and VP of sales. Naturally, if you have other executives you deem equal to these positions you should include them. The goal here is to keep the group as small as you can and your meetings short. The purpose of the meeting is this:

- Make sure this group agrees on the accuracy of the reporting metrics. Sounds simple but in my early years as a facilitator, I don't know how many times I would start a session only to have the VP of sales and the CFO get into it in front of a room full of people over what the gross sales were for the prior year. Having this group understand the metrics and agree on the accuracy of the reports that provide the metrics is of paramount importance.

- Ensure your governance is clean and up to date on every level, and offer this group an opportunity to surface any potential hot spots that might exist that need to be cleaned up prior to your off-site meeting. For example, I was halfway through a planning session with a major pharma group and there was a discussion by one division head who thought we were not spending time leveraging his product group. No one had bothered to tell him that his lead income generator lost its patent protection halfway through the prior year. Oops.

• Begin to discuss in very broad terms current challenges, current successes, economic conditions, and potential opportunities. This is where you begin to have your team step up and look at the global business climate rather than the task of day-to-day management. Have them read printed reports on operations/finance/HR/sales, discuss your industry, and discuss your enterprise in terms of your relative position. Ask a million questions and what answers they can't give you, have them go out and do some research before next week's meeting to get them. Discuss your debt position and banking relationship; read the audit report together, review the sales pipeline and the accounts receivable. Look at write-offs together, read some exit interviews and discuss your human resources needs and look for the "why" in everything.

• In July and August spend time meeting one-on-one with board directors, or in small groups for lunch. Find out in a relaxed environment how they are feeling about the economy, your progress, any expectations they might have for you or your team. Listen to their counsel, advice and opinion, gather information in small batches, and then see how it shapes up when you put it all together. If the majority of the directors think you're in for a tough economic near-term, running in to offer them a monster growth year and asking for debt or capital to do it probably wouldn't make much sense.

3. Goal setting should be complete by mid-August. By that time you will be close to finishing eight months of production and the metrics should be showing you trends with which you should be able to facilitate some reasonable predictive indicators when annualized and compared to trailing two or three years performance.

As the CEO, it is your responsibility to fix the overarching goals for the organization. They may not change a lot on an annual basis unless you have a major area of interest or a particular department that needs special attention. This might be infusing an acquisition goal or the selection and implementation of a major enterprise system. It should be something of significant and unusual size that requires extraordinary human or financial capital, or something that would have a major influence/impact on your corporate culture.

Here are some tips that will help this process and make it a bit more palatable for you and your team.

• An organization will have a difficult time executing more than four goals, with three being an optimal number.

• A goal should be simply stated, measurable in context, simply written, and direct to the area of concern or opportunity. It should not be defining in how the goal is to be accomplished. The goal should have approximate dates associated with operating rather than implementation dates. (This is a bit tricky but something that is critical to outcome.) As the CEO, you want to state when the company should begin to feel the benefit of the effort; you should not be directly concerned about when the associated actions are implemented. Here is an example:

GOAL 1. ACQUISITION IN HAND

The company will undertake action to ensure that it will attain incremental growth of 20 percent through the acquisition of a like enterprise no later than January 1, 2019.

Let's dissect this a bit. What could one denote from reading this goal?

- The boss wants us to grow by buying one of our competitors.

- The competitor must be around 20 percent of our volume.

- We need to get this done prior to January 1, 2019.

What did we not get?

- The boss didn't tell us how to do it, which means it's up to us.

- The boss didn't tell us who or where to get it, so that's up to us.

- The boss didn't tell us how much to spend, so we'll have to figure that out.

- The boss didn't tell us who was in charge, so we'll have to figure that out.

- The boss didn't tell us if we are to continue to grow organically. (Great clarifying question for the CEO.)

The idea here is that you set the goals and it will be up to them to figure out how to get this done and come back to you with a plan. Many CEOs believe that they should set the goals and then tell everyone what to do and how to get there. Wrong. Hire the best talent and turn them loose, they will most likely do a better job than you would, and they will be fully vested in the process and the outcome. Remember you always have veto rights. That's your job and responsibility if you see something going off track.

- Once your goals are written, they should be presented to the board for approval prior to your off-site meeting and before your budgeting process begins. I found that it was best to keep this out of a quarterly board meeting, as there was too much temptation to muddle around with editing. I presented these via e-mail and asked for a response with any questions and a yea vote, if they were in concert with me. I would note and respond to any concerns and move on.

- Make sure you have a discussion with your facilitators and give them your goals as far in advance of the meeting as possible. Great facilitators will drive you to clarity and ensure the presentation of your goals is spot on.

4. How to conduct the session. Every CEO and every organization will have a cultural methodology for off-site meetings. In my tenure as a facilitator, I've seen everything from resorts in Aruba to camping and white water rafting, hiking and repelling in Arizona to a dude ranch in Northern California. My opinion as both a facilitator and as a CEO is that this is a working off-site meeting and not a boondoggle trip. Both are meaningful trips just not necessarily at the same time. If I am sitting in a meeting room at a beach resort and can see everyone else out enjoying themselves when I'm expected to be inside working on business, you're probably not going to get my best effort. Conversely, if you don't plan some down time during your session, everyone has a headache by the end of the first day and can get bored with the whole thing. Great facilitators have tricks in their bags that help the participants stay focused while not wearing the team out.

Having facilitated more than 300 strategic planning programs as both CEO and consulting facilitator, I have seen and been directly involved with a wide variety of formats and timing. I have some recommendations based on my experiences, and if you have questions about any particular recommendation you can feel free to e-mail me and I'll offer additional information. (Or apologize profusely for steering you in the wrong direction.)

- Optimal length of meeting: two-and-a-half days

- Optimal number of attendees: ten to sixteen

- Travel in on Wednesday morning. Start session at 1:00 p.m. on Wednesday and go through Friday afternoon, adjourning around 4:30 p.m.

- CEO and facilitator should arrive Tuesday night to review facility and conduct a short meeting to ensure any last minute details are understood.

- Your room should not be near anyone else's.

- The meetings should be scheduled to run from 7:30 a.m. to 5 p.m.

- Dinner should be taken together and early to allow team to relax together or by themselves after dinner.

- No one arrives late or leaves early.

- No one is late for a meeting; buddy them up and have them be responsible for each other arriving on time.

- All meals should be planned and booked in advance.

- Executive admin should check everyone in, provide the agenda, and be ready with keys and information on meeting schedule, meal places and times, and transportation.

5. Recommended facilitation structure. Continuity from year to year is of paramount importance for getting your team through the process with an outcome that is worthy of the expense of the session. Experienced facilitators can keep you on target, on time, and get those results, even if session modules change due to the time one module might take over another. In every session I have ever been in as participant or facilitator, there is always some breakthrough thinking that the team wants to chew on for a while. That's to be expected. Here is a general timeline that may help you outline your session:

Day 1: Wednesday 1:00 p.m. – Convene
Welcome – CEO
Session Agenda – Facilitator

- Rules of Engagement
- Logistics
- Explanation of Session & Define Expectations

1:45 p.m.
Goals & Short Briefing on State of the Company – CEO
Read the goals. The CEO may take questions here but I recommend she only answer clarifying questions or questions concerning interpretation rather than entertain any "how" or "why" questions. At this point the CEO is making a statement

that should be interpreted as, "Look, it's my job to set the goals. It's our collective job to figure out how to achieve them. I'm going to help and I want a voice at the table, but I want to hear what the best talent on the planet in our industry has to say. That's what we're here for."

In my years I've rarely found a CEO who will say exactly what you want her to within the time frame you set, but if you can get close to this, you're a winner. Believe it or not, it is rare that a CEO has this entire assembly in front of her with no real agenda other than what's on her mind, so it's tempting to use the pulpit and most of them do.

Short Review of Mission – Vision – Values – Facilitator and Team

Where we are today and where we have been:

- Finance – CFO
  Current year and three years trailing Gross Revenue & EBITDA, any anomalies in the finance department

- Sales – VP Sales
  Current year and three years trailing booked sales, report on any anomalies in the sales department

- Operations – COO
  Current year production and three years trailing production numbers and report on any anomalies in operations

- Human Resources – VP HR
  Headcount for current year and three years trailing and report on any anomalies in HR

This is approximately a fifteen to thirty minute exercise. The purpose of reporting on these metrics is simply to ensure that everyone is on the same page relative to organizational performance and productivity. Early in my career, I was always amazed to learn that key executives could not tell you how many employees the company had or what the prior year's revenue was. In other cases, the COO and the VP of sales would get into it over the sales verses production numbers and the session would become an argument between these two over who was right. A strategy session is not about conflict. It's about creativity, cooperation, and commitment. Any potential conflicts should be cleaned up prior to the start of the session.

The purpose of these meetings is not to showcase anyone's PowerPoint, oratory, or presentation skills. I expect a one page handout from each executive with the numbers and information requested above and that's it. The entire exercise should take no more than half an hour total and provide the baseline and trends for review and reference when necessary throughout the session. Thus if we decide as a result of hearing our goals that the plan is to grow revenue by 22 percent, we can quickly calculate what that hard number is and conversely, if we are going to raise headcount by 5 percent, we know what that number is.

At this point in the session we have already accomplished some good stuff. We know where we're headed, we know where we've been, and you can bet everyone in the room is thinking about what those goals feel like. You can also bet that the radio station WIIFM ("What's In It For Me?") is wailing loudly in everyone's head. Mostly, people should be getting a bit jazzed up.

2:15 p.m.

Break for fifteen to thirty minutes and let the troops check messages, etc.

2:45 p.m. Reconvene

Rather than dive into the business, I like to make things a bit more personal and also head off any conflict that is inherently imbedded in the system between departments or executives. I like to bring in a behavior communication piece like DiSC or Myers-Briggs, as there is nothing like learning a little bit about yourself and the other people in the room. I prefer DiSC as it's a consistently validated instrument and a great facilitator can make this an enjoyable experiential exercise as well as a learning module. I'm usually good to spend an hour or maybe a bit more on communication so that the differences in delivery by all parties is understood and not taken personally. If you can refer to the way another person says what they have to say with a better understanding of the why in it, the whole room becomes a bit more forgiving. Some people like to think about things a bit before they speak while others can set a world speed record for answers with a two word statement. The important thing is to have the benefit of engagement from everyone and that requires a better grasp and understanding (sprinkled with a bit of forgiveness) for different behavioral communication styles.

4:00 p.m.

Driving Forces As They Are Now

Our next module is driving forces, an exercise to define business drivers as they exist in the business at this moment. This is a good reconnection with the information that was delivered earlier by our executives, only now, we are going to put some collective flesh on the bones. In this exercise, participants can be broken up into groups of four or five, each with a flip chart. The purpose is to identify those internal forces that at this moment make the business move forward — backward — sideways. In other words, what are we doing that is great for us, what things are we doing that take us in the wrong direction, and what are we doing that causes us to just tread water. These issues can be positive or negative, planned or unplanned, inherent in our industry, whatever. Just get them down on your flip chart and let's spend half an hour collectively debriefing on these important forces.

A word of caution here: Conditions out of our control are not a basis for business drivers. Business drivers are those things that we do over which we have control; conditions are external challenges and we have little or no control over their occurrence. A poor economic climate is a condition, not a driver. The same goes for who is elected as the president of the United States, even if those kinds of issues directly affect your business. Your job is to outperform these conditions by creating goals and subsequently executing sound strategies over which you have complete control.

You can list these and talk about them; you can stack rank them as to level of influence they have over the business; you can look for any commonalities and coincidences. You might even make some decisions to stop doing some things that don't work and start doing some things that might help you.

Your facilitator should be working hard to help you dig into these ideas and work through some healthy resolutions and or reward acknowledgement. Spontaneous celebrations are always acceptable.

An example might look like this:

Driving forces as they are now:

1. Communication
2. Manufacturing
3. Social Media
4. Leadership
5. Product Development
6. Marketing
7. CRM System
8. Centralization
9. Profits
10. Training

5:30 p.m.
Exercise Debrief, Wrap Up and Adjourn

Day 2: Thursday 8:00 a.m.
The facilitator should review the prior day's productivity and discuss what worked, any changes the group agreed to, what commitments were made and who made them, and a brief overview of what to expect today. A quick refresher on the behavior piece learned in day one, and a short experiential exercise provides a positive start to the day.

8:30 a.m.

Best Decisions

Breaking into small groups again, the participants are asked to look back through the current year and the four years trailing and make a list of the single best decision the company made in each year. The group may only select one per year. This exercise has many meanings. First, it quickly becomes a learning experience in company history for the newcomers while giving the more seasoned employees an opportunity to relate some important historical information based on their experience. That exchange can help cement company culture between the participants. Second, we can often get down on ourselves for not moving fast enough or putting up with things we know we shouldn't. This exercise gives us an opportunity to realize that "Hey, we did some great things and we made some great decisions together." That feels good to everyone.

This exercise should be debriefed collectively and each group should stand and deliver their five best decisions listed by the year in which they were made. There will most likely be some similarity to the lists but there may be some differences as well that need to be discussed and smiled about.

Take Backs

This is the Yang to the previous exercise's Yin. We break into groups again and discuss those decisions that, if we could, we would take back. This can be a bit rough, because we don't want to call them out as bad decisions because, truth be told, we may still be engaged in that behavior. So the exercise can be a bit interesting to facilitate, but keep in mind that the goal here is to get the group to recognize that there may be some things that we entered into that didn't pan out as we originally thought they would. Let's acknowledge them and own up to them and perhaps even make some agreements not to do them anymore. In addition to letting these decisions surface, it can also be helpful, with the right facilitation, to explore how these decisions made it to implementation. Potentially, this may be a flaw in the design of their previous decisions and it then might be practical to create a decision making model that everyone can agree on.

I recommend that you do not tarry at this exercise but rather, move through it. Like all exercises, if the need arises, I have learning modules that I can pull out and teach if the team lacks, say, a decision making model. It pays to plan ahead and be ready if the team needs the help. Education is a key component to great facilitation and great session outcomes. If I pull out my decision making model, show them how to use it, immediately tailor it to their needs, I always ask for a "treaty." I consider a treaty an agreement that once entered into, is binding to the participants. Thus, if we can reach consensus on a decision-making model, the team all agree to use that process going forward. I record all session treaties and review them with the team, either in follow up meetings or by e-mail to ensure the participants remember the treaties they made at the session.

10:00-10:30 a.m. Break

10:30 a.m.

Contemporary to the Times: Organizational Relevancy

In this next module, the collective team is asked to define some general business sectors that are important to their success and to their culture. These would naturally include finance, human resources, sales, and operations but can include any key department the group feels has significant influence on the business today. For example, you might have an unanticipated outcome when your core customer service group decides to share customer purchasing data in real time. It may have had a very positive outcome when your production staff steps up to fill orders they can see ahead of them. A challenge might be that your current operating system may be too slow to support the concept.

Once the list is defined, the participants split up into small groups and "press" the following question against each identified sector. The "press" is based on participant skill, education, and experience individually as well as the collective intelligence the team has.

1. Are we contemporary to the current market in this sector?

2. Is this business sector relevant in today's business environment?

One of the keys to facilitating this exercise is to have organizational "holes" identified and discussed relative to their importance. I'm going to offer you a few examples, as this exercise can get fuzzy if participants don't get the drift.

Example 1. The company has no social media program and if it is decided that there is relevancy to having one, the team has identified a potential "hole" in their organization. Conversely, if a company has always contracted for print ads with a marketing consultant, they may want to re-think that project in favor of the social media program.

Example 2. The company has always had a commission compensation program in place for the sales professionals. The competition has chosen to pay a higher base salary and a small commission program and your company is losing some of its best sales people to this competitor. Is your company contemporary in its sales compensation policy? If the answer is no, then you've identified a "hole" that needs to be addressed.

Example 3. Your medical insurance has been with the same carrier (through a good friend of the CEO) for many years. Recently, you have not been able to attract some much-needed talent to your company. Is your benefits plan the reason?

Example 4. You have a design engineering group that still works on ink-to-paper drawings for its research and development team when computer-aided design (CAD) has now developed to the point where ideas can turn to product in days. The team, however, is used to their process and enjoys the interaction of reviewing hard drawings together. Is the group culture relevant and contemporary? Or is the practice the differentiator between you and your competition?

Example 5. Is the company supportive of career development? Is it the company's responsibility to ensure that from a skills perspective the management team continues to develop their talents?

Allow this discussion to roll along and see how many "holes" they come up with where either the current sector is no longer relevant or necessary, or that it needs to become competitive in today's environment by moving to the next level. Sometimes our processes, procedures, skills, equipment, and general resources just become outdated or left in the organizational dust while we move on to other things. This is the place where we identify those areas that need additional management attention.

This exercise may open up some new thinking when it comes time to develop the strategic initiatives to support the company goals and these small "holes" may have to be cleaned up either as a matter of strategy or perhaps simply as a matter of corporate governance. Review and record this "hole chart" and park it until later on.

12:00 p.m. Lunch

1:00 p.m. Reconvene
Driving Forces As They Should Be
This exercise is the beginning of the search for organizational strategy. The group is tasked with the responsibility of defining what business drivers would exist if the company performed at its most optimal level in as close to a nirvana state as possible. For the purpose of this module, the facilitator should remove

any reference to the prior exercise of defining drivers as they are now. This is not meant to be simply a reverse or correction of the prior exercise but rather an opportunity to completely redesign their drivers to create a utopian environment that would allow for super achievement. It is also a good time for the facilitator to re-read the goals as the team needs to decide what drivers are relevant and necessary to their achievement.

For this module, the participants should again be divided into small working groups of five to six, armed with their flip chart and markers. Each team should discuss their ideas of utopian drivers, match them up against their goals and stack rank them for importance. This should be about a sixty minute exercise allowing time for creative thinking, discussion and stack ranking. It is important for the groups to define why the driver would be important and also the level of importance in the stack rank.

The facilitator should reconvene the participants as a whole and debrief the exercise by allowing each small group the opportunity to present their ideas and their stack rankings. The facilitator should then consolidate the list and the collective participants should stack rank the final list. There will naturally be some similar ideas that need to be culled into one final definition, so a little bit of give and take is necessary here.

An example might look like this:

Driving forces as they should be:

1. Communication
2. Profitability
3. Culture
4. Acquisitions

5. Education
6. Sales/Organic Growth
7. Technology
8. New Products/Services
9. Go Green Footprint
10. Geographic Expansion

Once completed, the facilitator should retrieve the list of driving forces "As They Are Now" and post the lists side by side and encourage a general discussion on the differences between "As They Are Now" and "As They Should Be" and the necessary bridges that need to be constructed in order to move from one side to the other. What do we need to do in order to reach utopia? The facilitator may not choose to have a long discussion about this but rather place the question in front of the group and ask them to think carefully about how this might happen and why it would be positive.

Example:
Driving Forces As They Are Now
1. Communication
2. Manufacturing
3. Social Media
4. Leadership
5. Product Development
6. Marketing
7. CRM System
8. Centralization

9. Profits
10. Training

Bridgework: Activities we must engage in to reach utopia

Driving Forces As They Should be
1. Communication
2. Profitability
3. Culture
4. Acquisitions
5. Education
6. Sales/Organic Growth
7. Technology
8. New Products/Services
9. Go Green Footprint
10. Geographic Expansion

3:00 p.m. Break

3:30 p.m. Reconvene

Strategic Initiatives

Strategy lives in the space between what you have and what you want. Strategic initiatives are those large actions that need to be taken in order to achieve your goals. Strategy can change; it can speed up or slow down or stop altogether. It can be parked to let a larger missive pass and then continue on. Strategy must have a driver; it cannot succeed on its own. Strategy must have fuel in order to move, with fuel defined as tactical pieces of labor and task that must be completed in the proper sequential order in order to be fully utilized.

Strategy must be measured because we always need to know if it's working properly and therefore we need to know where we started and where we are on the journey at all times. Strategy must have strength, but strength without purpose is useless. Therefore strategy must target a goal. Strategy should not be overutilized on any one goal and thus balance of strategy is important to goal achievement. There must be a balance of strategic initiatives to support all organizational goals equally. Conversely, if an organization is overlaid with too much strategy there will not be enough fuel to have any of them gain traction.

Typically, if each goal is supported by two active strategic initiatives, that is enough for any organization to take on at any given time from both a human and financial capital perspective. As I mentioned before, the optimal goal number is three so with some quick math, it's easy to see that coming out of this session, the team will have three common goals, and potentially six strategic initiatives. That is a huge undertaking for any organization, large or small; if you can affect the overall success of the business by implementing six pieces of strategy, one can easily see how this process can take an organization from good to great. It's not just about good customer service or throwing people off the bus. It's about facilitating and executing visionary goals with profoundly impactful strategic initiatives.

The facilitator should review the information above and convey these concepts and recommendations to the participants.

There should be a discussion between the teams to ensure that everyone understands the process.

1. Break up the participants into small groups of five or six. Attempt to arrange the groups so that they are cross-disciplined as well as comprised of varying degrees of tenure with the company.

2. Take goal one and read it again to the groups. Review the metrics as presented by the executives at the start of the session, review the "Holes" list, review the driving forces "As They Should Be" list. Have the groups work on the single most important activity the company must complete in order to achieve the greatest impact on the goal. Each group should attempt to come up with three or four. Stay away from tactical work. Getting a report to measure the sales pipeline is a tactic, but reinventing the sales culture of the company is strategy-worthy and may be necessary to organically growing the company 20 percent over the next two years.

3. Allow one hour for this exercise. Reconvene as a team to debrief the exercise by allowing a representative from each group to present their strategic initiatives in the order of perceived impact as well as defining the "why" behind them.

4. Once complete, combine any that are alike from the different groups and create one set of strategic initiatives listed under goal one.

5. Repeat the exercise for all goals.

This exercise will take you the better part of day two, and two hours into day three.

Day 3: Friday 8:00 a.m.

Review all modules from day one and day two. This is not to bore anyone but rather to solidify in their minds the work and collective reasoning that they have produced together as a team and an opportunity for all of them to take collective ownership of both process and product. When the team leaves the session, the individual participants should feel both vested and party to the outputs.

Setting the Strategy

The goals should be up on the wall and listed below each goal should be the various strategic initiatives. While some goals may have more strategic initiatives than others, that is not important at this stage of the process.

Each participant should be given a sticky note pad. On the initiatives listed under each goal, each participant should mark their number one and number two choices by simply writing the number one and then two on separate sticky notes and placing the sticky note directly on the initiative. This is called a "gallery walk" and most facilitators are familiar with the exercise. This should take approximately thirty minutes.

Once complete it will quickly become apparent which strategic initiatives are preferred by the team. The facilitator should then rewrite the goal, then list the strategic initiatives in order of the team's selection. The participants take a time out and clear the room. The facilitator then reviews the information with the CEO and allows the CEO an opportunity to either vet the strategy as presented or make changes as she sees fit. This is about gathering information democratically but the acceptance ultimately must be the decision of the CEO.

In more than twenty-five years of facilitation, I have never seen a CEO change or alter the team's choices for strategic initiatives. This process allows for everyone's voice to be heard and in the session, it is legitimate for anyone, including the CEO, to argue their point with everything they've got. Therefore, it is and has been highly unlikely that any concept would get this far along without the CEO's approval and agreement.

That said, the formality of having this time to quietly review the strategy without the pressure of the group present, should be a courtesy the team understands and accepts as a privilege afforded the CEO, who will ultimately be held responsible by the board for its execution.

This should take no more than fifteen minutes and then the team should reconvene.

Here is an example of what this product should now look like.

GOAL 1. ACQUISITION IN HAND

The company will undertake action to ensure that it will attain incremental growth of 20 percent through the acquisition of a like enterprise no later than January 1, 2019.

G.1.1. Strategic Initiative Code Name: "Snake Doctor"

We will design, build and implement an acquisition guide and subsequent process that will be used as a roadmap to acquiring a competitor that will grow our business 20 percent by January 1, 2019. The guide will include, but not be limited to, all tangible and intangible processes that will be involved in acquiring a competitor from identification of the target through the final merge or absorption of said target.

Okay, so what do you see here? You've got your goal that you have seen in front of you for the entire session. The last exercise tells us that most likely this team has never made an acquisition, so their strategy is to build a process and a guide to get there. Good thinking. This is where most people stop, and this is why most strategic planning has good creative thoughts but is never implemented.

Reconvene the Team

The CEO should make a statement at this point that compliments the team on their creativity and hard mental work it took to get here. This is hard thinking work if it's done right and these initiatives should be the best that can be had in your company and in your industry. The CEO should make a formal statement of acceptance of the team's strategic initiatives. Now the really hard work begins.

Assignment of Authority and Responsibility

Taking one goal and one set of strategic initiatives at a time, it is now time for assigning responsibility for acting on the strategic initiatives. The team discusses the initiatives one at a time and collectively decides and agrees on which executive should be the "sponsor" of the initiative. (Remember the goals are the responsibility of the CEO.)

Each C-suite executive should act as the sponsor for at least one initiative. A sponsor has ultimate authority and control over the initiative and the associated work that is assigned in order to complete the initiative. The sponsor has the authority to deploy funds, assign tasks cross-functionally, set schedules, and create timelines. The sponsor may choose to run several projects under his assigned initiative and as such may select project managers and project teams to get tasks done. The sponsor is responsible for meeting all timelines and milestones and reporting back to the team on a pre-determined schedule.

The only person who has the authority to change timelines or milestones is the CEO.

At this point, each goal has two or three strategic initiatives to support it and a sponsor to manage it, who has both the authority and responsibility to see it through to fruition. It is a good time now to have a five minute free-for-all on each initiative. This is facilitated by having the sponsor and facilitator stand at the front of the room and take notes on every comment every participant has. The participant goal in this exercise is to help the sponsor identify any concerns, ideas, comments, or suggestions the folks have on his initiative. At this time, participants may also offer their services as a committee member on the initiative.

Here is an example of what the product looks like at this point.

GOAL 1. ACQUISITION IN HAND

The company will undertake action to ensure that it will attain incremental growth of 20 percent through the acquisition of a like enterprise no later than January 1, 2019.

G.1.1. Strategic Initiative Code Name: "Snake Doctor"
Sponsor: Duke Jones, EVP COO

We will design, build and implement an acquisition guide and subsequent process that will be used as a roadmap to acquiring a competitor that will grow our business 20 percent by January 1, 2019. The guide will include, but not be limited to, all tangible and intangible processes that will be involved in acquiring a competitor, from identification of the target through the final merge or absorption of said target.

Comments:
"We should make a list of all competitors who do at least 20 percent of our volume."

"We need to figure out how we get the money to buy someone."

"I think we better talk to our attorney and learn how to do this."

"How do we ask someone if we can buy them?"

"Are we going to fire all their employees? I wouldn't like that."

"If they have a VP of HR and we do too, who will get the job?"

"What's the tax deal on buying someone?"

"Will their products be the same as ours?"

"How long will this take? We'd better get this done quickly if we're going to meet the deadline."

Sue: "Hey Duke, I'd like to help on this. I worked on the legal stuff on an acquisition at the last company I worked for."

Pete: "Me, too. This is the exciting part of the business."

You get the drift. Everyone gets to have a shout out and the information can go a long way towards helping the sponsor get their arms around their initiative. This is all about getting traction and action toward your goal. Duke now has some interested lower level executives who want to help, and he found out Sue even has some experience he can tap into. Sounds like two potential project managers for Duke.

There are two critical actions that the CEO now has to work on in order to ensure this process and her goals are taken seriously.

• Each C-suite sponsor should have a portion of their annual "At-Risk" compensation tied directly to the implementation of his or her project. Note that I said "implementation" rather than "success." The fact is, no one knows whether or not any strategy is successful until it's deployed. There are times when our entry level assumptions don't pan out. What happens if there are no competitors out there that we can afford? That's not the sponsors' fault. Getting the strategy implemented on target and on time is what they should be compensated for.

• Junior executives at the AVP, director, and GM levels should be working with a sponsor on an initiative. As the CEO, I would encourage this involvement and support their work effort by allowing them to participate. I would also find a way to reward these folks with some financial or personal recognition of some sort. These are your future senior executives and they should be involved as much as is possible.

There will no doubt be questions on the use of project management as a tool to assist the sponsor in formatting their strategic initiative that allows for tracking of tactical work and process flow. While I support such an idea, I have a small word of caution here: I have seen instances where the use of project management software can stall a project and a team by making the process so detailed it implodes. I recommend a simple two or three page document that is supported online that allows team members to freely update progress on their deliverables and is transparent to all team members. (I do not recommend a thirty-page project management document.)

At this point in the process you now have a collective understanding of:

- Our historical performance metrics

- Our goals as stated by our CEO

- Knowledge of how we communicate differently

- What drives our business today

- Where we have "holes" that need attention to be relevant and contemporary

- What we want our business drivers to be

- Strategic initiatives that will take us to our goals

- Sponsors who are responsible for strategic initiative implementation

- Support from the collective team body to achieve them

Our session is close to its conclusion, with two more modules to complete.

COMMUNICATION LINK

The communication link is the way and means of communicating what transpired at this session to the core of employees that were not privileged to be in attendance. Remember when you were in a junior role and you would hear about these meetings? The only real benefit I typically enjoyed was my boss wasn't around for a few days. I never heard a thing about the meeting and rarely was I ever included in a debriefing of any kind.

I recommend that the communication link be discussed in open forum and the team decides what information can be shared and how it will be shared. I recommend that the CEO be directly responsible for the delivery of the information to every employee in the company. This means a face meeting where she stands up and delivers the goals and whatever piece of strategy and discussion the group has agreed is appropriate to disseminate. I further recommend that the team take at least a moderate stab at the specific points as well as the methodology for what is to be disseminated. The responsibility for delivery of the content, however, cannot be delegated; it must come directly from the CEO's mouth.

The point to take away from this exercise is that no matter which participant is asked what happened at the session, they should all be saying the same thing and walking the same talk. There should never be any dissention between participants as to what went on and what was agreed to. A decision by one must be supported by all and vice versa.

PERSONAL COMMITMENT, CONTRIBUTION, AND RESPONSIBILITY

The final piece of the off-site session is gaining a commitment from each participant as to what they have learned and what their level of commitment is to the content they have developed. I call this "standing and delivering" and it can be a bit emotional. I ask each participant to take a turn standing in front of the room and reading their biggest take-away from the session as well as what their personal contribution will be to the plan. I ask them to write down what their personal commitment is and what their responsibility is to ensure the successful implementation of the goals and initiatives. By the way, I collect these documents and keep them for reference throughout the year.

(Special note: The CEO is the last person to stand and deliver.)

At this point, your session is complete. Looks easy, right?

CHAPTER 12

The Board

I have served on a number of boards in my life, in public, private, and government sectors and they are as dynamic and interesting as each sitting member is individually. I have been paid to sit, mostly unpaid or with small stipends, and sometimes with just direct meeting expenses. My experience tells me that the amount of money you pay a board member does not necessarily translate to either competency or quality of the director. There are many lessons to be learned in how to work with your board while still trying to run a business and the first is to determine how much control you have over the selection of the directors, the chairman, and/or committee chairs. If you have none, you might want to rethink the contract I talked about in Chapter Two. If you have a selection process in place, you need to understand where you are in that food chain. And if, like most companies, there isn't really anything in place and you have no real process, design one. You're smart, you'll figure it out.

Believe it or not, most organizations have a difficult time finding members or directors that are contemporary and knowledgeable enough to actually contribute something of worth, not to mention committed enough to prepare themselves for service to your organization. In my experience, most organizations spend little if any time interviewing and getting to know potential board members, as it is usually a referral from a business associate, banker or attorney; someone they know and trust. There is not often enough time spent understanding business philosophies or background work to see if the experience they bring to the table creates organizational value.

A board selection should be treated with the same, if not a greater level of scrutiny than you would apply to the selection of any other C-suite executive. Aside from the usual background and character references you would ask for, it is important to understand the skills and experience a candidate brings to the equation. What is their motivation for taking a position on your board? Some see this as a prestigious position, some do it for the money as a retirement gig, and some have a genuine interest in helping you help your business. My advice here is to think carefully about the skill sets and behavioral approach of your current board. Are you overloaded with generalists, perhaps financial folks, or attorneys? Anytime the input balance is upset on your board, you're in trouble. The same is true about your business in general. Think about this: Would you want six sales specialists on your executive team and no financial people? Or how about three human resources VPs and no operations representative? You couldn't run a business that's out of balance, and you can't run a board that way either.

As a consultant, I always encouraged my CEO clients to

build out a full orientation program and, in fact, go deeper and build an assimilation plan, which is a completely different animal. Typically, we sit new employees down with someone from HR and we run through the employee handbook—maybe. We go through the health benefits plan, the 401K plan, and the holiday plan—maybe. We might even show them where the washroom is. Then we turn them loose to go about their business because human resources people are always very, very busy. This is not what I'm talking about.

An assimilation plan calls for continued support and guidance until a new team member is fully on board. They know the layout of the building, where good lunch places are, what the unwritten rules are, where and why the meetings take place. A solid and interested mentor should be assigned to support introductions all around the office and arrange lunch or coffee with different team members until the newbie is comfortable and able to function without assistance. The same is true of board members. Assimilate them, don't just orient them. We need to understand that these folks are smart and they have worked a lifetime, but they may not be familiar with your industry or your manufacturing process or your sales CRM software, and good directors want to understand everything. The more they understand, the more they can help you apply solutions to challenges and that's why they are there. Conversely, let's not forget that a new director has an obligation to learn as much about your business as possible and should be willing to put in their own time in order to accomplish just that. Every meeting that goes by where you are explaining how your business operates rather than seeking creative solutions is one more missed and costly opportunity.

I get a lot of questions about my expectations of board members, including about things like fair compensation and time required to serve. Generally, if you are of size, rule of thumb says once you hit twenty-five million in gross, you ought to be paying about a hundred thousand in total board fees, distributed between all directors. Some are higher and a lot are lower; just remember you get what you pay for, but more crucially, what you ask for. Concerning time, a director needs to plan on 200 hours of contribution time and one day a quarter of board meetings. Depending on the size of your board, fees would go up or down per head based on the total number of directors that are dividing up the pool. Typically the chairman puts in more time and gets a bigger slice, as do the audit committee chair and the compensation chair. I'm hearing average board fees in larger operations ($100 million and above) are around $80,000 for each director. It is typically not acceptable to pay operating executives for serving on their company board.

One of the challenges we have with so many investment bankers and equity partners running around buying up businesses today is that boards are becoming overloaded with financially centric directors, while the industry expert, the operations professionals, and the sales and marketing folks are left out. Then we wonder why our CEOs are turning over on the average of every eighteen months and not sticking with engagements. You can only take so much financial pressure to perform before you can't run your business any more. Bless the investment bankers because I work with a lot of them, but show me two of them that can discuss supply chain management or executive leadership development and I'll eat my hat. They can talk that talk but in my experience few of them can walk it.

Case in point: Like every other business executive in the world, I belong to several investment banker and equity partner groups. They love to find industry professionals with a few bucks to invest and hook up with them. It lends credibility to their portfolio and in turn, they get a lot of freebies out of you. You have to agree to look over deals in your area of expertise and you get a nice dinner once or twice a year with some pretty smart folks. You also get to participate in some interesting deals and occasionally you're asked to sit on a board. Most of the time for free, mind you, but nevertheless it gives you a feeling of control over your investment. That's when everything goes well.

So one of the groups I'm in makes a successful run at a services organization. Like most of these deals, the transaction is usually for one reason and that's to purchase an undervalued company that is poised to grow, throw some money at it, force feed growth (usually they like it to be organic), and spin it in thirty-six to forty-eight months for monster returns.

As it turns out, I get a board seat with the new group and at the first meeting, everyone is giddy with delight; the owners, who are still there working and hold four board seats, are now pretty rich in addition to having some growth money in the company war chest (provided by debt of course), courtesy of the new investment bankers. The investors are happy because they believe they bought a jewel for down money, and the future looks bright for everyone. That lasted for less than half the year, or two board meetings.

Within six months, the new board is overpowering a

basically family-run business. They are spending money on crazy expensive accounting and governance because that's what investment bankers know how to do. One of the previous owners, now a paid executive in sales, is doing the classic "I'm in a jam" mode, overpromising and underdelivering and the board is sick of missed projections coupled with a difficult attitude. The gal is nasty, aggressive and not afraid to get into it with her board. Not the brightest turnip in the patch, the gal has been running things her way for many years and now she's got a bunch of investment banker guys in her face telling her how she should be running it and she's having nothing of it. Oil and water.

I could go on and on about that one but the lesson here is that you must have a board that you can work with. Not when everything is going well, but when the chips are really down, how is everybody going to behave? Will they give you a heads-up even when they are not supposed to before the crap hits the fan? Will they take care of you no matter what? Do they get your business and can they have a seriously positive impact on how you look at your business? If you are constantly dragging them along with you its most likely time to find some new folks. For those of you entertaining the financial concept of shouldering up with an investment banker, equity partner group, or venture capitalist, take your time; there are some great ones and there are some not-so-great ones. When you see the suits coming in the door, the first questions you ask are, "Have you ever run a business before? Frontline, CEO or presidential position?" If the answers are no, keep looking.

It's very important that both your audit committee chair and your compensation chair have real life experience with accounting and compensation. A great audit chair can really help you map out tax and capital strategy in addition to asking the right questions of your CPA firm at the annual audit. Respect the fact that these folks get jazzed about digging into the detail of the numbers and take the time to slow down and listen to their input. Compensation is tricky; you want to get what you deserve and if your philosophy is at odds with your compensation committee chair it can make for a very tense relationship. I strongly encourage the use of an outside neutral compensation consultant to help you reach agreements on executive compensation working hand in hand with you and your chair.

The most important point here is this: Despite what people think, a board seat isn't like being the Pope; you don't get to stay there until you die. My recommendation is to swap out board members every five years so that you don't get any relics snoring their way through a compensation meeting. Five years is enough time to have someone educated enough to help you, and also long enough to get out of them what you need, and remember, balance of input is of critical mass to you. Current economic conditions, industry changes, politics; almost anything can change your input needs so always remain flexible and contemporary with the people who serve you, as when things change, so should you.

Another interesting aspect of board make-up is the age and gender of its members. In my entire life I don't think that I have witnessed more than one board that had members where the average age wasn't mid-to-late-sixties at the youngest side (most average much older), and only on very rare occasions did I serve with a female director.

Women think differently than men, and if you want to see how far we have progressed in the workforce, just take a gander into the board rooms and you'll still see there is an overwhelming number of white older gentlemen and a lot of "good old boy" tradition going on. One thing that always served me well in moving through as many industries as I did was casting the net way beyond what the company was used to in seeking new talent. Rather than just thinking about diversity, I encourage you to take it on as an organizational goal. Nothing wakes up an organization like inserting a non-traditional director onto the board that is made up of an inbred team of people who have been sitting in the same seats for twenty years. It wakes everyone up and ultimately, if you make a good pick, it can lift the organization up. Conversely, without your support and without making a good selection, it can become a revolving door with a lot of "I-told-you-so" along the way. While carrying some inherent risk at the onset, diversity can ultimately take you to new ways of looking at old problems, which in turn, present opportunities that may never have surfaced.

I feel that America needs to reach out to female executives for board seats, and it needs a much larger dose of female and minority CEOs that understand what it's like to actually operate a business in today's global climate. While there is much to learn from aged executives, if you are out of the firing line for more than five years, you may have lost some edge. Business is moving and changing too rapidly today, and the way we solved challenges five years ago is ancient history. Technology alone creates communication change that now has customers able to maintain their own raw materials supply chain needs inside your organization. That wasn't an option two years ago. Try to explain that to a seasoned executive who has not worked in a business for five years and is now a sitting director on your Board as you attempt to explain and use an app your team just developed. Of course this is a gross generality, and there are exceptions, but don't lose the message— keep your director seats full of contemporary and diverse people who can help you get where you want to go. If you're 100 years old and maintain your edge, remain contemporary to the technology and bleeding edge pace and magnitude of information we have to deal with today, God bless you and serve well.

I know, I know, I'll get hate mail from dozens of senior directors, and I apologize in advance to all of you contemporary folks who are the exception to my experience. So, to vanilla this up a bit, let me simply say that the net needs to be cast far and wide and never limit your options based on any prejudice or predetermined theory you might have or might have inherited. Let your directors know that it is not a job for life and what your terms of endearment look like and what your philosophy is relative to their expected input and influence on the business.

CHAPTER 13

Good Luck on Your Journey

You can't write a book about being a target without first acknowledging all the transgressions you caused to put the target on your back in the first place. Today in America, business leaders are under greater scrutiny, a greater threat level, with more regulations, personal transparency and more personal exposure than ever before. In fact, I would go so far as to say that leadership itself is under attack, and directly in the line of fire is the chief executive officer, president, or top whatever it is you call the guy or gal that literally has his or her back to the wall when counsel shows up with a subpoena.

It's not about "the buck stops here" anymore; in fact, in many companies directors love the guy that loses money but never drives the organization to be better, stronger, or faster—as long as they don't create any controversy. Most people like that because it doesn't rock the boat, doesn't upset the status quos. And in America, we've grown very familiar with the status quos. In fact, I feel we often revel in it. We even legislate it and mandate it whenever we can without too much hassle.

We should have big signs at our borders that say, "America: The Land of the Status Quo." It's safe and warm and we don't have to work too hard to keep that feeling. We are becoming complacent leaders that are more concerned about not making a mistake, living the regulations, executive oversight, and the legalese that dominate our board meetings, and thus in turn, run our country. We believe that we can continue to tax the hell out of businesses, allow regulation to control all natural resources, and that we can run an economy purely on service and high tech development while production manufacturing is better done offshore.

Every day our televisions blast reality shows by the dozen, creating false images of the person at the top. I love the incognito boss, the undercover stuff, and the "You're fired." I wish business actually worked that way, and I'm sure there are people out there who believe that crap. But just consider that if you only have four hundred employees, or you're a franchise and people don't recognize you, you're already pretty screwed up from a leadership perspective. I've worked in many larger organizations and I can tell you that everyone knew me and spoke to me, shook my hand, and asked me questions. To try fooling them (even without the mustache) would have been ridiculous. When you start handing out cash to employees who have a sick mother, or who have not taken a vacation in twenty-something years, or have lost a loved one to cancer, you damn well better have some extremely deep pockets, because they are a daily occurrence millions of times over. To think that anyone has to go undercover to find that out is so crazy it's crazy.

I'm not saying that as a CEO you don't get hit up every day with those kind of stories and requests, because it's part of the job; you just don't have to go undercover to find them. Trust me, they find you, and they aren't ashamed to ask. In my years I have been hit up by everyone from senior executives to the receptionist for personal loans. The number who have paid me back is one. Five years after the fact, a secretary to whom I had lent $1,500, actually sent me a check and I was so thrilled, I tore it up. The amount of "expectation" money I have personally lent employees over the years is well in excess of the money they talk about on the reality shows. Oh, and on that subject, you don't get many thank you notes.

Our legal system is one of continuous improvement; more specifically, self-perpetuation. There is always someone with a complaint, someone whose life isn't what it's supposed to be (or isn't what his or her spouse thinks it should be) who is ready, willing, and able to take down the CEO, because as God is their witness, they have been done wrong. The truth is, we give them the target on our back. We stood up in front of everyone, we took out the red paint and we painted it thick and round and placed that huge red dot right in the middle of our back the day we accepted the position. Then we try to drive business, and the people who work there, to outperform the economy. We consolidate jobs, we replace people with technology, we try to reduce our cost of labor at any sacrifice, and we try to drive fixed costs out of our organizations. And we wonder why people consider their work environment "hostile." Hostility is baked into the system.

The minute we accept the role of the chief executive officer, expectations change, even though we didn't. We are suddenly expected to be pillars of our community, at church every Sunday, generous philanthropists and above all, immune from the normal challenges of life. Our CEO getting a divorce? An affair? Oh my God, someone making that much money and they do that?

Listen. We will continue to do the things that make us human, just like everyone else. We're human and we make mistakes. The difference is our mistakes are unforgiveable. The difference is the more money you make, the more righteous you are expected to be. It is interesting that the only time people think you're worth a penny is when they get a raise, or the stock goes up on retirement day. If you start believing your "self-stock" is ever more valuable than on your hire date, you're dreaming.

I was speaking to a relatively young executive who had recently retired after his company was bought out by a larger competitor. He lamented that he had no succession plan and that the business was getting tougher and tougher as it grew, and he didn't want the pressures of hiring additional staff and putting his accumulated wealth back to work in the business. I asked him what had made him as successful as he was and yet also made him want to cash in at so young an age. His response shocked me. He said that he was tired of living every minute, making every decision, as if he was going to be on the six o'clock news.

I was a C-suite executive for almost twenty-five years and have been the guy with his back to the wall for the majority of my business career. My transgressions are long and deep and there is no penalty for "piling on" so I'm sure some folks who know me will add to my list and call me out for things I'm guilty of, the ones I've forgotten, or the things they thought I did. My apologies for not remembering I slighted you, broke your bubble, fired you, or lied to you. Because I've done all those things and a lot more, justifying that I was building and protecting the long-term health of my business and therefore delivering shareholder value. I've plotted long-term strategies to remove seasoned executives and weaned many companies of the dependence of Peter-principled executives who thought the company owed them for what they had done in the past, not what they could do in the future. I've beat my hands on the table, called people out in front of others, and one time even had the board I was working with create a motion and subsequent directive against the CFO to get him to balance an inventory overage.

I've worked for private sector companies, public sector, family owned, government and even an employee stock ownership plan (ESOP) once, so I've seen and heard a lot of stuff. I have engaged with other CEOs my entire career; learning, counseling, coaching, and mentoring them as they grew the targets on their own backs. The unique thing about my career is that I was able to cross business sectors and was never pigeon-holed into one industry. I worked in consulting, a couple of stints in medical device manufacturing, service based businesses, security, and agriculture. I've worked for really big companies ($300 million), some mid-size ($30 - $100 million), and some start-ups. In all industries there are two things in common: first, the target on your back grows in direct proportion to your authority; and second, the same business principles apply in any business no matter the sector and no matter how uniquely the sector perceives itself.

Here's the scary part: I was enormously successful in spite of the kind of person I was or the mistakes I made. This is due to one simple fact: nothing got in the way of shareholder return, profitability, or the bottom line. I built unstoppable teams, I educated people, I trained them to be self-sufficient, taught them to execute on dreams and strategy alike. I taught them how to make decisions, to be good deal makers and good partners once the deal was done. I created fortunes for at least two of the companies, was involved in numerous industry changing acquisitions and built over a hundred careers at all levels that are still viable and strong to this day, all working-like-crazy people building the targets on their own backs.

Every day we see more and more norms being thrown out the window. It is all a CEO can do to keep up with the demands of both directors and shareholders alike, let alone run a business with any sense of normalcy. Most, if not all financially centric industries have a similar challenge; they have a lot of money and no place to spend it as business continues to constrict and play a close-to-the-vest game relative to debt.

The experience many investment bankers and equity firms had from the late 1990s through the early 2000s finding and attracting companies seeking high growth seed money is no longer the case, and this has investors working extra hard to find potential targets. With money to lend, traditional banks are being a lot more forgiving and the trend now finds them working hard to maintain the accounts they enjoy by loosening covenant restrictions and minor violations when reasonable to help their clients stay on track. Mind you, the reason they are doing this is because it is more restrictive to lend new money than ever before and the prospects for any loosening of commercial credit requirements in the near term is not a reasonable bet.

The other fascinating result of the influx of investment banker and equity funds as finance vehicles for growth and related capital needs is that the make-up of governing boards has been for a long time leaning towards financially centric directors who are not elected for their operations expertise, industry knowledge or marketing prowess. Rather they are appointed to keep a watchful eye on the money and if you follow that belief, their singular focus is on financial performance and return on investment. In days past, a board director was elected based on skill, education, experience, professional discipline, or area of expertise and it was a competitive market with organizations both public and private seeking to gain the best advantage and best talent to assist their respective management team.

I was recently sitting in a board meeting with a high tech company and there were five board members, two observers, and two members of the executive team—the CFO and the vice president of sales. Over the course of a four-and-a-half-hour meeting, three hours and ten minutes were spent going over financial information. We went through every detail of accounts payable, service call detail, and margins by account. We covered all accounts over thirty days in accounts receivable and we revised and reviewed projections for next month and accounted for any budgeted item out of a plus or minus 3 percent range no matter the dollar amount. It was crazy. More important however, is that to the men in this room, this was normal.

I would surmise the average age of this board is around fifty and all but myself were investment bankers and equity players. I'm an operator, and have been for more than thirty years. I initially invested in this company because of the brilliance of the young man who founded it, and also because I understood the business model as it is specific to my work history. I was angel money and content to help this very young team navigate the challenges I knew they would face in the start-up years because I had done the same thing. I knew how to market this company, I knew what their service record would look like and I knew beyond a shadow of a doubt that their capital expenditure budget was too light. With my experience, I had a lot I could and did contribute to the board when we were in the angel stage.

As soon as we grew to the next level and the second tier of necessary financing came around, the makeup of the board naturally transitioned to where it is today. As I became a minority shareholder the new investors were nice to me and offered me a continued director seat. Although my investment is still intact I decided that the game of numbers wasn't for me. The company is doing well and growing like a weed but I daresay it's still due to the tenacity of the founder, not the numbers crunchers. The sad part here is that, while this young CEO is making it, he's not getting the benefit of mentorship and guidance that helps develop young executives into the kind of leaders this country so desperately needs.

People join boards now for several reasons: some like the seemingly stern seat of power and prestige, some actually want to contribute and help organizations and their leaders grow, and some just want the money. No matter the motivation, it would be nice to see organizations work as hard to attract good contributing board members as they do attracting capital. Additionally, it would be nice to see the capital providers reach out to candidates who can contribute to the overall health and well-being of the organization and its leadership. I believe until we get this straightened out we will continue to see the highest rate of turnover in history at the CEO level. According to Booz Allen Hamilton, the global average of CEO tenure is just 7.6 years, down from 9.5 in 1995, with two out of every five CEOs failing in the first eighteen months of service.

The new paradigm of leadership has become impossible for mortal man or woman to live up to. When every decision we make and every action we take personally or professionally is completely exposed to a worldwide audience for judgment, eventually few are left to lead. We have forgotten we are mortals, not gods; we have great ideas, we have transgressions, we love fiercely and we often make emotional decisions. Sometimes the same passions that drive us to lead companies to great success are the same passions that, when turned to our personal lives, cause disasters and vice versa. Is it more important to count one's marriages or the shareholder value a CEO brings to the equation? What is important and relevant to one's leadership contribution? Why do we worry about the gender or gender preference of our business leaders? Why are we still fighting the battles for equality in the board rooms of America? As a CEO, what is your obligation to bring enlightenment to your operation?

That said, if you're expecting perfection from these chiefs, either personally or professionally, if you're expecting them to somehow live their lives as the righteous few, you're forgetting that we are human and therefore have the potential to disappoint, just like every other human being on earth.

Being a CEO is not always pretty, but it is a hell of a game and I love every freaking minute of it. Good luck with your journey. Never, ever quit, no matter what happens.

To contact the author please email ed.jenks@thejenksgroup.com.